ELIMINATING MINOR STOPPAGES
ON AUTOMATED LINES

ELIMINATING MINOR STOPPAGES ON AUTOMATED LINES

Kikuo Suehiro

Case Studies compiled by:
Takuo Fukuda
Director, CIM Promotion Center
Tokai Plant
Hitachi, Ltd.

 **Productivity** *Press*

Originally published as *Chokotei kaizen no susumekata* by the Japan Management Association, Tokyo. copyright © 1987 by Japan Management Association. English translation by Bruce Talbot copyright © by Productivity Press, a division of Productivity, Inc.

Productivity Press
444 Park Avenue South, Suite 604
New York, NY 10016
Telephone: 212-686-5900
Fax: 212-686-5411
Email: info@productivitypress.com

Library of Congress Cataloging-in-Publication Data

Suehiro, Kikuo, 1939-
  [Chokotei kaizen no susumekata. English]
  Eliminating minor stoppages on automated lines/Kikuo Suehiro: case studies compiled by Takuo Fukuda: [English translation by Bruce Talbot].
      p.   cm.
  Translation of: Chokotei kaizen no susumekata.
  Includes bibliographical references.
  ISBN 0-915299-70-4
  1. Assembly-line methods. I. Title.
TS178.4.S8813   1992   91-33701
670.42--dc20   CIP

02 01 00 99 98   10 9 8 7 6 5

Contents

Publisher's Message

More and more automated equipment is being incorporated into production processes. Although this trend solves certain problems, it creates others. Automated equipment is usually required to perform very specific tasks at high speeds, with delicacy and precision, and without human intervention. In many cases it is also required to diagnose problems or even to self-correct. As complexity increases, so does the probability of error.

When this equipment is linked to other pieces of automated equipment and then tied in to a carefully orchestrated, computer-controlled factory automation system, then errors, however slight, can have a tremendous impact. This is especially true when the equipment must be stopped, even briefly, to effect the necessary repair. The increased reliance on machines compels industry to ensure that they function properly. Equipment improvements are actually improvements to the production process itself. This book describes a step-by-step procedure for eliminating a certain type of problem in automated equipment — that of *minor stoppages.*

When new automated equipment is installed, it often must be adjusted and even modified to ensure that it operates automatically in a manner consistent with the production process in that particular factory. The author, Mr. Kikuo Suehiro, states that more than 85 percent of defects addressed by the type of improvement efforts he describes are initial defects in the equipment itself. Certain design problems in a new piece of equipment become obvious only when it is actually used in production. Mr. Suehiro also points out that equipment improvements are short-lived when production must be changed to accommodate a new product model because this creates a new set of conditions with its own unique problems. Equipment modifications and improvements are, therefore, ongoing activities.

To help the reader understand what minor stoppages are, Mr. Suehiro dedicates the first two chapters to defining them precisely, and outlining various methods for accurately measuring the frequency of their occurrence. The importance of these two chapters cannot be overemphasized. In the next three chapters, he describes the reasons for reducing the frequency of minor stoppages, and discusses his unique approach to such an improvement program—an eight-step procedure designed to force the user into an intense study of the minor stoppage phenomenon in the search for causes and the appropriate corrective action. A chapter is dedicated to each step. Be assured that, if followed in accordance with Mr. Suehiro's instructions, this procedure will result in the required improvement.

Although the focus of the book is narrow, the issues with which it deals are broad. The procedure described is an intense one that requires skills in data collection and analysis as well as an ability to solve problems creatively and a desire to get to the root of a problem. It requires a knowledge of basic equipment technology, and if that knowledge is lacking, it requires the ability to find it and learn it. To be effective, it also needs an environment in which there is cooperation among the various departments concerned with the equipment. But more than this, it requires machine operators who possess the skills necessary to assist in the equipment improvement program.

Training equipment operators in basic skills and in specific job-related tasks must form an integral part of an overall company policy. Equipment technology will inevitably change, and operators must be able to keep pace. They must have the ability to learn, solve problems, think creatively, and contribute to an information pool that will help develop better, more reliable equipment. The input of operators becomes vital in the search for solutions to equipment problems and production issues. In addition, manufacturers of automated equipment, in their efforts to make machines that require fewer adjustments and improvements following installation, must incorporate input from production and maintenance personnel as well as from engineers.

However, it is important to understand that any improvement program such as the one described in this book cannot be implemented effectively without the support and encouragement of management. This is also true of the basic TPM system that forms the foundation for these improvements: it is essentially a top-down activity.

This book forms an integral part of an ongoing series from Productivity Press on the subject of TPM. These books discuss the basic philosophy and concepts of TPM, and describe practical step-by-step procedures for effective implementation at all levels of a company. Titles for other books in this series are listed at the back of this book. *Eliminating Minor Stoppages on Automated Lines* was originally published by the Japan Management Association, and describes one of the improvement tools available to a factory that has established the basics of TPM with the support of upper management.

For making this book accessible for an English-speaking audience, our thanks go to Bruce Talbot for providing an excellent translation; Bruce Graham for editorial development of the text and for redrawing the characters in the cartoons created by Keijirō Kaitō; Christine Carvajal, copyediting; Maureen Murray, proofreading; and Elisa Abel, indexing. Finally, thanks to project manager Susan Cobb and the production team of Daniel Rabone and Gayle Joyce. Also thanks to David Lennon for the cover design.

Foreword to
the Japanese Edition

MINOR STOPPAGES AND FACTORY AUTOMATION

To remain competitive in pricing and quality, and to ensure profitability, manufacturing companies are introducing automated equipment and developing factory automation (FA) systems. However, when factories bring in new equipment that is supposed to operate automatically, they often find that it is not as automatic as it was supposed to be. When a large line of such equipment starts having little problems here and there, it can become extremely difficult to maintain steady output. If this equipment forms part of a large-scale FA system, these little problems can add up to major difficulties in maintaining productivity.

For example, consider an FA production line that consists of 100 machines and that has a production output of 10,000 units per day. If the average equipment failure rate is only 0.1 percent (1 failure per 1,000 operations), it means this 100-

machine line would experience about 1,000 failures each day. Even if it took an average of only 30 seconds to fix each failure, that would still be a total daily maintenance time of 30,000 seconds, or 500 minutes, or 8 hours and 20 minutes. If the failures occurred one at a time throughout the day, they would keep one person quite busy fixing them. However, it must be assumed that the failures will occur randomly and thus that at least two people will be needed.

Even such minor failures will prevent the factory from achieving its daily output of 10,000 product units unless there are adequate buffers between the processes or enough slack in the "takt" time* of each equipment unit. In this example, the equipment has a reliability rate of at least 99.99 percent or even 99.999 percent.

Next, there are various factors to consider such as defects in the system or in individual equipment units, operator errors due to inexperience, lack of maintenance preparedness, and so on. But solving all of these problems is still not enough. Something new is needed, what might be called "a new concept of improvement." Lately, manufacturing companies have been searching for this new concept as they try out different types of maintenance programs such as TPM.

IMPORTANCE OF IMPROVEMENTS
AIMED AT SLIGHT DEFECTS

There is an immense variety of production processes being used in factories, and they have several common characteristics.

First, production equipment in general consists of anywhere from several hundred to several thousand components.

---

* Takt time is the time required in minutes and seconds to produce a component or set of components. It is calculated by dividing the total daily operating time by the total daily quantity of products sold. Takt time is subject to periodic change.

Such equipment turns out good products only when all its components are in good condition and operating normally. Second, the equipment will not operate normally unless it is receiving the proper amount of energy in the form of electricity, compressed air, oil, heating fluid, control signals, and so on. In addition, each of the following factors and elements must be in proper order: materials, environment, and equipment operation.

Thus, production involves the mutual operation of millions of elements. These elements represent an almost limitless number of production requirements, and it is only when everything is working together in just the right fashion that the factory can continually turn out good products at the proper speed. This also means that in every factory there exists the potential for countless defects and abnormalities. In view of this, it is obvious that production requirements cannot possibly be met without some kind of active intervention. However, the daunting task of maintaining countless production elements is not something that can be dealt with simply — for example, through basic maintenance programs or general improvement measures. To deal with them effectively, you must closely examine each of the several dozen or several hundred problems encountered, then systematically take corrective measures against each of them.

Individual defects in equipment often go unnoticed or overlooked. When encountering slight defects in automatic equipment, the operators often deal with them simply by "lending a hand" to the equipment, and thus the defects are not brought out into the open as real problems. It is important to realize that even in large equipment units or large-scale production lines, overall improvement comes as an accumulation of improvements designed to eliminate slight defects. So, instead of ignoring them, factories should make slight defects their primary focus.

THREE IMPROVEMENT ELEMENTS

The elements shown at the three corners of the following triangle are the three key elements for making systematic improvements. If any of these are omitted, you cannot expect to obtain good results.

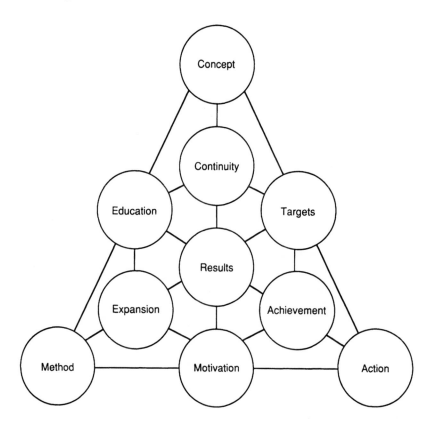

The improvement activities described in this book constitute an excellent method with a well-balanced emphasis on all three of these elements. There are examples that show how the *concept* and *method* of activities designed to reduce minor stoppages are put into practice. Having studied these examples, the reader needs only to provide the third key element of *action* and the results are sure to be positive.

This is not to imply that such action will be easy, for it will probably be just the opposite; in fact, it is no exaggeration to say that it will push people to their limits. With the problem of slight defects, it is especially important to make continual improvements, and this requires a good understanding of the *concept* element.

By performing activities to reduce minor stoppages under Professor Suehiro's guidance you learn the importance of carefully observing current conditions in the factory. These activities begin with a visit to the work site, where you meticulously observe the conditions and other phenomena related to minor stoppages. Doing this alone reveals a surprising number of problems. As this book describes in considerable detail, observing current conditions from a variety of perspectives will speed up progress in making improvements.

In the course of our own improvement activities with Professor Suehiro at Hitachi's Tokai Plant, we set target values that were remarkably high by conventional standards, such as a frequency rate of once every 20 minutes, or a 20-fold increase in mean time between failures (MTBF). Without exception, we reached those targets. Since then, we have made similar diligent improvement efforts in various workshops at our factory, and each time we have achieved the same high target values. The key to this success has been the concept of taking thorough measures against slight defects.

Having practiced these improvement methods under Professor Suehiro's guidance, we became inspired to spread these concepts and methods to other factories throughout the industry. We told Professor Suehiro of our wishes, and he found the time to write this book. This is probably the first book that systematically explains the improvement measures required to solve the problems of minor stoppages and slight defects. As such, it is an important book that will no doubt contribute much to industrial development.

Takuo Fukuda
Director, CIM Promotion Center
Tokai Plant
Hitachi Ltd.

Preface

This book grew out of efforts to integrate the production process in order to promote factory automation, shorten lead times, and increase productivity. As part of our equipment improvement efforts, we set the target of reducing the frequency of minor stoppages to $1/20$ or less of their current level. We have managed to reach this improvement goal in more than 100 equipment units.

Mr. Takuo Fukuda, director of the CIM Promotion Center at Hitachi's Tokai Plant, encouraged me to write a book about these kinds of improvements. I was very much impressed with the wide range of approaches taken by the Hitachi employees and by their diligence in making improvements. I am also thankful to Mr. Fukuda and others at Hitachi for their assistance in preparing some of the case studies presented in this book, and also to Mr. Fukuda for his insightful foreword on the promotion of factory automation and the reduction of minor stoppages.

The term *minor stoppages* expresses a rather vague concept that has very different interpretations, depending on where it is used. However, in today's factory, automated equipment is becoming increasingly more sophisticated, so the central problem to which the term refers is equipment stoppages caused by errors in automated processes. In view of this, this book takes the following approach to minor stoppages.

1. It focuses on error-related stops, especially parts handling errors in automated machines and automated lines.
2. It uses mean time between failures (MTBF) as a measurement criteria for evaluating minor stoppages.
3. It describes thorough improvements based on case studies where the MTBF for minor stoppages was increased by a factor of 20 (that is, the stoppage frequency rate was reduced to $^1/_{20}$ its former level).

Improvements are not easy to describe, but the more concrete and specific the improvement is, the easier it will be to understand. However, if the improvement is very specific, it may be meaningful only to those people who work with the same process. On the other hand, if the improvement deals with commonly used approaches and procedures, it cannot be very specific or concrete. Still, if anything is going to help the reader deal with the myriad types of minor stoppage phenomena, it is the common approaches and procedures.

If you take a cold hard look at a particularly troublesome problem that failed to admit of a solution, you usually find that the reason for the failure was that people did not really understand what caused the problem. Consequently, this book pays particularly close attention to the process of searching out causal factors. To make this process more understandable, I have selected a few case studies that presents a relatively pure example of that search. Some readers may feel that these case studies have nothing to do with the equipment stoppages at their own factory. However, the case studies presented here contain almost all the issues related to reducing minor stoppages. Obviously, no individual case can simultaneously deal with all the issues; however, all case studies are characterized by the same basic approach to problem solving. I only ask the readers to understand that, in selecting case studies for this book, I have chosen those that present the issues in a relatively simple and clear manner.

In accordance with the wishes of the companies involved, I have omitted the names of the factories and individuals that appear in these case studies.

Acknowledgments

Advanced automation is pursued boldly at Hitachi's Tokai Plant, and for that very reason, reducing minor stoppages is a serious issue at that plant. Their organized promotion of improvements has produced many successful results, some of which are described as case studies in this book. I would like to express my deep thanks to Superintendent Taosa Kubota of Tokai Plant and to all the others at the plant for their kind assistance. I would also like to thank the many people who helped with the case studies I selected from other Hitachi plants, such as the Toyokawa Plant and Gifu Plant, and from plants belonging to other companies as well.

In addition, I am particularly indebted to Dr. Masakatsu Nakaigawa, the creator of skills management, for teaching me his views and his approach to slight defects, and to the illustrator Mr. Keiji Kaido and publishing agents Hobun Tonomura and Eiko Shinoda of the Japan Management Association. Finally, I thank my wife, Yasue, for her long hours at the word processor.

Companies and Plants that Contributed Case Studies (in Alphabetical Order):

Hitachi
  Gifu Plant
  Tokai Plant
  Toyokawa Plant

Hitachi Metals
  Kumaya Plant

Minolta Camera Company
  Sayama Plant

Sekisui Chemical Company
  Shiga Ritto Plant

Part 1

Understanding Minor Stoppages

1

Definition of
Minor Stoppages

In 1967, the popular Japanese term for minor stoppages was *choko choko tomari* (literally, *sputter, sputter, stop*). Recently, this has been shortened to *chokotei (sputter-stop)*. In English, there are such expressions as *idling and minor stoppages, small line stops, intermittent stops, starts and stops,* and so on. The standard term in either language is still a matter of debate. In this book, the term *minor stoppages* is used to avoid introducing a new term, which would only add to the confusion.

THE MEANING OF MINOR STOPPAGES

The term *minor stoppages* expresses a rather vague concept. Its meaning differs greatly depending on the company or factory where it is used. Sometimes it refers to equipment breakdowns, and sometimes, especially in lines that involve a lot of manual work, it refers to equipment that operates on idle because an operator is late in completing a certain task. But strictly speaking, minor stoppages refers to neither of these. Today, when functions such as autoloading, process integration, and automatic detection of abnormalities are becoming increasingly more sophisticated, one of the main things to which the term refers is equipment stoppages caused by errors in automated processes. Therefore, this book deals primarily with minor stoppage phenomena that occur on lines of linked automated equipment, and defines a minor stoppage as follows.

> In automated equipment for which the specifications indicate that during normal operation the equipment operates automatically without requiring human intervention, a minor stoppage is (1) an equipment stoppage due to a failure or error in the automatic handling, processing, or assembly of parts or workpieces; or (2) an equipment stoppage due to the occurrence of a quality-related abnormality. In either case, restoring normal operation usually requires action by an operator to reset and/or reactivate the equipment, and this is usually all that is required to overcome the equipment stoppage.

In short, this book treats minor stoppages as equipment stoppages that arise from errors in automated processes.

SUPPLEMENTAL DEFINITIONS

Recovery by Resetting

People think of minor stoppages as small failures in equipment. But where do you draw the line between small and large equipment failures? Most people judge the size of equipment failures by the time needed to fix them, that is, the downtime. However, if minor stoppages are defined as equipment problems that take no more than say, five minutes to repair, the true meaning of the term is missed. In this book, time is not used as the measurement criterion. Rather, minor stoppages are defined as equipment stoppages that arise from errors in automated processes, and include the following three phases:

1. Workpiece flow stops
2. Operator resets workpieces correctly
3. Operator reactivates process

Error!

Thus, one of the main elements of the definition must be the operator's resetting action, and the error or failure must be the kind that can be repaired by this action.

Equipment Breakdowns

Although operational failures in automated equipment do fall into the category of equipment breakdowns, the fact that some require only a quick resetting action distinguishes them from more typical types of equipment breakdown problems caused by things such as worn contact points on limit switches, broken shafts, and worn packing on pneumatic cylinders.

Even though equipment breakdowns account for some portion of the causes behind minor stoppages, it is not a large portion. Therefore, it is necessary to recognize the role of equipment breakdowns without emphasizing it. However, further on in the book, in a discussion of methods to measure and evaluate minor stoppages, some cases are presented in which equipment breakdowns are the causes of minor stoppages.

Frequency Factors

The definition of minor stoppages should not include cases in which the equipment stops at regular intervals during normal operation, such as when materials are being supplied. Such stops do not qualify as minor stoppages. Instead, these cases should generally be considered under the concept of *frequency factors* because they are part of the equipment specifications. Processing errors, on the other hand, indicate how reliable that equipment really is. As factory operations become increasingly automated and accelerated, minor stoppages become an ever more difficult problem; newly introduced equipment must be submitted to successive improvement and control measures in order to prevent minor stoppages from becoming too frequent. In this sense, the number of minor stoppages can be a key indicator of successful factory management. So, even though frequency factors do not figure into a definition of minor stoppages, be aware of the relationship between the two.

Consider the case in which an abnormality occurs in a cutting tool during processing and, as a result, the cutting tool must be replaced. This is a processing error or problem and should, therefore, be counted as a minor stoppage.

Late Operations and Standby

When an operator is slow in finishing an operation, sometimes the equipment must go on standby until the operator is finished. In this case, the equipment itself is not functioning abnormally, so this delay would not be considered a minor stoppage. Other types of line standby that do not properly fall into the category of minor stoppages are secondary phenomena such as standby due to an error in an upstream or downstream process, or a slight standby due to a gap in the cycle time. These types of problems should be solved by measures such as speeding up the slow manual operations, correcting the error in the originating process, and making line-balancing improvements.

Other Types

Certain other types of line stops, such as end-of-shift stops, stops for retooling (for model changes), and rest stops (for nonautomated lines) are obviously not included as minor stoppages.

2

Measurement Criteria for Evaluating Minor Stoppages

To make improvements, you need current values, target values, and measurement criteria for evaluating the effects of the improvement. This is true not only in the world of business management but also in the world of specific technologies, where advances in measurement methods are prerequisites for improvement and technical progress.

NUMBER OF MINOR STOPPAGES PER DAY

There are advantages and disadvantages to recording the number of minor stoppages per day. In theory, nothing could be simpler than to keep track of how many occur. This figure serves as a good measure of improvement since the number of stoppages per day is a real number. High figures, such as 100 or 200 per day, also impress upon everyone how important a problem minor stoppages are. However, a simple record keeping system does have some disadvantages, which become apparent immediately.

For example, simply tracking the number of minor stoppages in a day does not reveal several important factors, such as how much time was spent that day in fixing the stoppages, how much overlap there was between rest time and automatic operation time, and how many other equipment problems occurred (such as breakdowns) because of changeover or other causes that do not belong to the minor stoppage category.

In other words, this minor-stoppages-per-day figure does not accurately reflect the operating time of the target equipment.

MINOR STOPPAGES AND MTBF

In 1974, company K adopted the MTBF (mean time between failures) measure as a tool for improvement activities on its fully automated production line, which was based on American technology. The company has been using the MTBF measure ever since.

MTBF is a reliability engineering term that means the average amount of operating time between the occurrence of breakdowns that require repairs. In this instance, *repairs* are those made by maintenance actions after the start of equipment operation. The MTBF is in inverse proportion to the breakdown rate. The breakdown rate can be defined as the relationship between breakdown occurrences and the continuous operation of an item such as a system, subsystem, machine, device, component, part, or element. The breakdown rate helps determine reliability.

Figure 2-1 illustrates how to calculate the MTBF.

For the equipment under study, OT represents the overall operating time (a period such as a day, week, or month) and Nf represents the total number of breakdowns during the OT. The MTBF can then be calculated using the following formula.

$$MTBF = \frac{OT}{Nf}$$

Higher MTBF figures indicate higher equipment reliability. Use the MTBF figure as a general indicator of reliability, such as

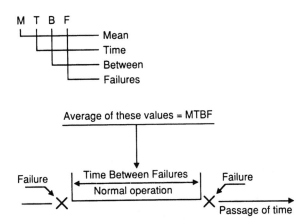

Figure 2-1. Mean Time Between Failures (MTBF)

when speaking of the 5,000-hour MTBF of robots at company U, or the 200,000-hour MTBF of electric power generators at company V.

The MTBF measure can also be applied to minor stoppages. In this case, the number of failures becomes the number of minor stoppages within the operating time period. Hereafter, unless otherwise specified, all reference to *MTBF* is to be understood as meaning *minor stoppage MTBF*.

Method for Calculating Minor Stoppage MTBF

Calculating the minor stoppage MTBF is quite simple, as shown in the following four equations. First, the basic equation:

$$\text{Minor stoppage MTBF} = \frac{\text{Operating time}}{\text{Number of minor stoppages}} = \frac{OT}{Nf}$$

Equation 1

where
OT = operating time (the time during which the equipment is operating with all required functions)

Nf = number of minor stoppages

Equation 1 should be used only if the Nf figure is 10 or greater.

The following three equations show how to calculate the MTBF per day (or shift), per week, and per month, respectively.

$$\text{Minor stoppage MTBF per day} = \frac{\text{Operating time per day}}{\text{Nf per day}}$$

Equation 2

$$\text{Minor stoppage MTBF per week} = \frac{\text{Operating time per week}}{\text{Nf per week}}$$

Equation 3

$$\text{Minor stoppage MTBF per month} = \frac{\text{Operating time per month}}{\text{Nf per month}}$$

Equation 4

Where

In Equation 2, the Nf per day must be equal to or greater than 10.

In Equation 3, the Nf per week must be equal to or greater than 10.

In Equation 4, the Nf per month must be equal to or greater than 10.

The minor stoppage MTBF figures used in Equations 2, 3, and 4 are for operations that include line stops such as end-of-shift stops and changeover stops that are not really *minor stoppages*. So an MTBF figure of 1,000 minutes does not necessarily represent 1,000 minutes of uninterrupted operation. Instead, it means that minor stoppages occurred Nf times within an operating period that may have included end-of-shift stops and changeover stops.

Cautions Concerning Measurement Periods

One condition for using the preceding four equations is that the Nf figure must be 10 or greater. Suppose that, in the case of Equation 2, where the MTBF is calculated every day, there comes a day when there are no minor stoppages at all. In this equation, an Nf value of zero would produce an MTBF value of infinity. This does not mean there is something wrong with the equation; it simply means that the day-based equation is not suitable for calculating the MTBF in this case. At this point, lengthen the measurement period and switch to Equation 3, which is a week-based calculation of the MTBF, or to Equation 4, which is month-based (see Figure 2-2).

Measurement period = daily

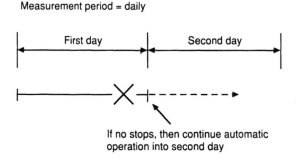

If no stops, then continue automatic operation into second day

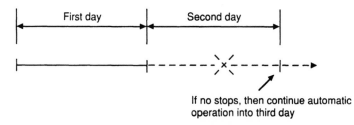

If no stops, then continue automatic operation into third day

In this case, the minor stoppage MTBF measurement period should be lengthened to one week or one month.

Figure 2-2. Minor Stoppage MTBF and Measurement Periods

DATA COLLECTION

Operating Time (OT)

The best kind of recorder is a mechanical counter. There are two types: those that count the operating time and those that count the downtime. For MTBF recording, it is better to use an operating time counter; however, there is a problem with this recording method. Standby time, which is neither operating time nor downtime, will get mixed in with operating time unless you use a counter signal to prevent this from happening.

If there is not much fluctuation in cycle time, you can measure the actual cycle time (ACT) and obtain the operating time using the following formula (Equation 5).

$$\text{OT (Operating time)} =$$
$$\text{ACT (Actual cycle time)} \times \text{Nk (Number of processing work-hours)}$$

Equation 5

This formula is not applicable in the following situations.

- Situations in which a mechanical counter cannot be used
- Situations in which the following detector signal conditions exist:
  - standby time is mixed into the operating time count
  - only downtime can be counted, even when problems at adjacent processes create frequent *slight standbys*
  - other cases where the use of the recorder is not effective

Number of Minor Stoppages (Nf)

To count frequently occurring minor stoppages the use of a mechanical counter is the preferred method because experience has taught that handwritten records are rarely reliable. This is because whenever a minor stoppage occurs, the first thing the operator does is fix it. Recording it is secondary. As a result, from one-third to one-half of the stoppages go unrecorded. Typically, the factory worker in charge of the recording process will estimate that about one-third of the minor stoppages were not recorded. Often, however, when a mechanical counter is later introduced, the worker is surprised to find out that about 70 percent of the minor stoppages had actually been omitted.

The best kind of mechanical counter to have is the kind that counts only the minor stoppages (that is, error-caused stops). Fortunately, many of the newly developed types of automated equipment include automatic control circuitry that provides error signals specifically for such error-caused stops.

At company A, the line supervisors developed an on-line device for measuring, calculating, and displaying the MTBF (see Figure 2-3). Since this factory specializes in electronic circuitry, developing this direct automatic MTBF counter was probably a simple matter.

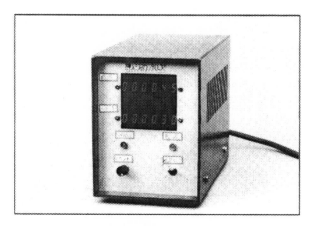

Figure 2-3. Minor Stoppage Counter

If the counter merely counts the number of line stops and cannot distinguish between those which are error-caused (minor stoppages) and those which are not, you must find a way to calculate the number of minor stoppages.

Use the following formula (Equation 6) to calculate the number of error-caused minor stoppages based on the total number of line stops counted.

Nf (Number of minor stoppages) =
Total recorded line stops − Line stops not caused by errors

Equation 6

As shown, subtract the line stops not caused by errors from the total recorded line stops. Line stops not caused by errors include the following.

- End-of-shift stops.
- Rest stops. (Only when automatic operation is not planned during the rest periods.)
- Changeover (for new models). However, any stops for changeover that must be done in response to a broken

tool or jig or other equipment problem must be included as minor stoppages.
- Frequency factors.
  - Stops for feeding in materials or for removing processed goods.
  - Stops for routine replacement of blades and other tools.
  - Stops for routine quality checks (for example, as specified by QC process plan).

Among the frequency factors, the only ones that should be considered *line stops not caused by errors* are those which occur at a frequency that is required by such things as equipment specifications or quality standards. This means that all stops made for retoolings and quality checks in response to particular problems rather than as part of routine maintenance should be included as minor stoppages, that is, stoppages caused by errors.

Consequently, it is better to calculate the number of frequency factor stops on the basis of the number of processing work-hours and standard frequency factor stops than it is to calculate it on the basis of ACT (actual cycle time).

To more clearly define minor stoppages, distinguish them from equipment breakdowns. However, when compiling MTBF statistics, include stops due to equipment breakdowns as minor stoppages. The main reasons for this are as follows:

- In equipment where minor stoppages are a problem, they occur much more frequently than breakdowns, so excluding stops due to breakdowns would have little effect on MTBF values.
- The statistics should be kept as simple as possible. If you can avoid having to make the distinction between minor stoppages and stops due to breakdowns, so much the better.
- The point of monitoring minor stoppages is to make corrective improvements. Therefore, if equipment breakdowns are too numerous to be ignored, improvements

should be made to increase the operational reliability of the equipment.

MTBF AS APPLIED TO NUMBER OF OPERATIONS

So far, the description of MTBF has been based on the assumption that the T (time) in MTBF is the kind of time measured with a clock, and that, in most cases, minutes are used as the basic unit of measurement. However, over the years, the use of MTBF measurement for minor stoppages has spread to the point where it is being used to compare various differences in process conditions. Consider, for example, what happens when trying to compare two pieces of equipment by using a one-hour (60-minute) MTBF measurement period.

- The first piece of equipment has an operation cycle time of 0.3 seconds, so there are 12,000 cycles within the MTBF measurement period.
- The second piece of equipment has a cycle time of 60 seconds, which means there are only 60 cycles within the MTBF measurement period.

Even though the MTBF measurement period is the same for each piece of equipment, there is a 200-to-1 difference in the degree of reliability being measured. Actually, since equipment that operates rapidly tends to have reliability problems related to errors during acceleration, the difference is probably greater than 200 to 1.

In studying reliability, the number of operations becomes a kind of *time* measurement, so it is correct to use the number of operations as a substitute for the T in MTBF when measuring and calculating failure rates. Referring back to the two situations previously described, you could therefore say that:

- An MTBF of 60 minutes becomes 12,000 cycles
- An MTBF of 60 minutes becomes 60 cycles

Number of operations

Therefore, there are some cases in which it is more appropriate to use minutes (or seconds) as the T unit in MTBF and other cases in which it is better to use the operation cycle as the T unit.

Generally, the time-based (minute or second) unit is more convenient for MTBF studies done from the perspective of factory work, such as measuring the reliability of equipment that is supposed to work automatically without any timing errors. On the other hand, the cycle unit is a more significant MTBF unit from the engineering standpoint.

If you are using both types of units, distinguish them as MTBF-min (for minute-based units) and MTBF-cyc (for cycle-based units).

MTBF IN AUTOMATED LINES

Sometimes it is necessary to measure the MTBF in stand-alone automated equipment, while at other times it must be measured in lines of connected (linked) automated equipment.

If 20 stand-alone processes that each have an MTBF of 60 minutes are linked to form a line, the line will have an MTBF of 20 failures per 60 minutes, or 1 error every 3 minutes. Obviously, there is a big difference between MTBF figures for stand-alone processes and for lines of linked processes.

Line MTBF

Although the distinction between *line MTBF* (MTBF for a line of connected equipment) and *process MTBF* (MTBF for stand-alone processes) has no significance from the engineering standpoint, it does help to more clearly identify the object that is being measured. Therefore, the distinction will be made in this book through reference to MTBF for a line of connected equipment as *line MTBF*, a term that is used by factory managers no matter how many individual processes are linked in the line.

Average MTBF ($\overline{\text{MTBF}}$)

$\overline{\text{MTBF}}$ is the average value based on the MTBF measured at each process in the line. Therefore, some of the processes will have MTBF values greater than the $\overline{\text{MTBF}}$ value, while other processes will have smaller-than-average MTBF values. As such, the $\overline{\text{MTBF}}$ is an abstract value rather than an actual (measured) value.

$\overline{\text{MTBF}}$ is expressed in the following formula (Equation 7).

$$\overline{MTBF} = \frac{\text{Operating time} \times \text{Number of processes}}{\text{Total number of minor stoppages}}$$

$$= \text{Line MTBF} \times \text{Number of processes}$$

Equation 7

$\overline{MTBF}$-min and $\overline{MTBF}$-cyc

A distinction can be made between $\overline{MTBF}$-min and $\overline{MTBF}$-cyc for $\overline{MTBF}$ measurements too. These values are indicated as follows.

$\overline{MTBF}$-min
$\overline{MTBF}$-cyc

MTBF and the Number of Processes

In Equation 7, there are difficulties involved in using the *number of processes* element. To begin with, it is not always easy to tell where one process in a line ends and where the next process begins. Furthermore, some processes are complex, while others are simple. The easiest way to divide up the processes in a line is to consult either the process configuration diagrams or the process equipment layout diagrams that were drawn up by the production engineers. Such diagrams will show the distinctions between processes, and this information can be used to measure MTBF values for each process.

EFFECTIVE CAPACITY UTILIZATION
RATE FOR EQUIPMENT

Reduction of minor stoppages is often used as a method of increasing the operating rate of the equipment. This section introduces the concept of *effective capacity utilization rate* for equipment.

Basic Definition

Dr. Masakatsu Nakaigawa, the creator of skills management, has proposed the following basic definition of effective capacity utilization rate for equipment.

$$\text{Effective capacity utilization rate for equipment} =$$
$$\text{Time-based operating rate} \times \text{speed-based operating rate}$$

$$\text{Time-based operating rate} = \frac{\text{Effective operating time}}{\text{Planned working time}}$$

$$\text{Speed-based operating rate} = \frac{\text{Theoretical cycle time}}{\text{Actual cycle time}}$$

UR-2 and UR-3

On the basis of Dr. Nakaigawa's definition, the following symbols can be used to permit a more detailed distinction between types of utilization rates.

Effective capacity utilization rate for equipment = UR
Effective capacity utilization rate for equipment 2 = UR-2
Effective capacity utilization rate for equipment 3 = UR-3
Time-based operating rate = TOR
Speed-based operating rate = SOR
Nondefective rate = R

When equipment is operating at full speed but is turning out defective goods, this cannot be called *effective capacity utilization*. A nondefective rate of 99.9 percent will have little impact on the calculations for the effective capacity utilization rate for that piece of equipment. However, if the nondefective rate of the equipment is about 95 percent, approximately 5 percent of the operating time is spent producing defective products, and this cannot be included in the effective capacity utilization rate.

This is why, when calculating the effective capacity utilization rate, the nondefective rate should be added as a third element in addition to the time-based operating rate and the speed-based operating rate. The symbols UR-2 and UR-3 represent the formulas that include the two elements and three elements, respectively.

These symbols are shown in Equations 8 and 9.

UR-2 (Effective capacity utilization rate for equipment 2) = TOR × SOR

Equation 8

UR-3 (Effective capacity utilization rate for equipment 3) = TOR × SOR × R

Equation 9

In addition, these elements can be calculated as follows (Equations 10 through 12):

$$\text{TOR (Time-based operating rate)} = \frac{OT}{WT}$$

Equation 10

$$\text{SOR (Speed-based operating rate)} = \frac{TCT}{ACT}$$

Equation 11

$$\text{R (Nondefective rate)} = \frac{Nr}{Nk}$$

Equation 12

where
OT = operating time
ACT = actual cycle time

WT = working time
Nk = number of processing work hours
TCT = theoretical (or target) cycle time
Nr = number of nondefective items

Both UR-2 and UR-3 must be correctly linked to the actual results of the measurement periods. Based on the definitions expressed in Equations 8 and 9, the equations for UR-2 and UR-3 are as follows (Equations 13 and 14).

$$UR\text{-}2 = \frac{\Sigma\,(TCT \times Nk)}{WT}$$

Equation 13

$$UR\text{-}3 = \frac{\Sigma\,(TCT \times Nr)}{WT}$$

Equation 14

In each case, the figure indicated as Σ is the total for the target model.

The correspondences between UR-2 and TOR or SOR, and between UR-3 and TOR, SOR, or R must be as shown in Equations 8 and 9.

3

Examples of
Improvement Results

As mentioned in the preface, there have been many cases in which a reduction of minor stoppages has brought excellent results. This chapter presents three such cases, each involving a different type of target equipment, as follows:

1. An automated line
2. A line using human workers and robots
3. Stand-alone automated equipment

SUCCESS WITH AN AUTOMATED LINE

An automated line at company A performs automated assembly of precision components (see Figure 3-1). It includes robots that automatically insert and extract parts, assembly robots, and other automated assembly equipment, and comprises a total of 12 processes.

Errors in automatic feeding of parts and errors in automatic indexing of very precise assembly positions are both regarded as minor stoppages. The aim of the improvement project was to improve the equipment TOR (time-based operating rate) as well as the operator's work efficiency. In addition, the improvement team sought to help the engineering staff improve the cycle time at bottleneck-prone processes. The improvement project brought the results shown in Figure 3-2.

Figure 3-1. Automated Line

The results are summarized as follows.

$\overline{\text{MTBF}}$-min: 30 times greater
$\overline{\text{MTBF}}$-cyc: 36 times greater
MTBF-cyc level after improvement: 40,000 cycles/process
UR-3: 2.3 times greater
Operator work efficiency: 4.7 times greater

Note: The fact that improvement in $\overline{\text{MTBF}}$-cyc was greater than improvement in $\overline{\text{MTBF}}$-min reflects shortening of the cycle time.

SUCCESS WITH A LINE USING HUMAN OPERATORS AND ROBOTS

An electronic equipment assembly line at company B includes some 60 processes, of which about 40 are automated

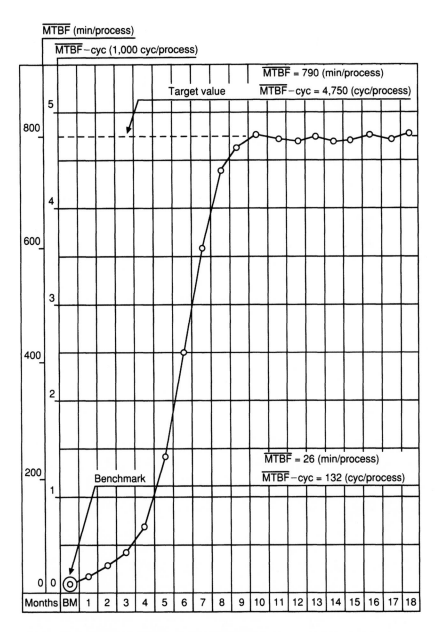

Figure 3-2. Results of Improvement Project (Average Values for 12 Processes in Automated Line)

including assembly, adjustment, and quality checking. It is a typical modern assembly line that combines human workers with robots and other automated equipment. The previous year, the productivity of the line (daily output per worker) was doubled. The improvement team took on the challenge of doubling productivity again this year. Their improvement scheme included two main goals:

1. Eliminating minor stoppages at robot processes and automated equipment processes
2. Getting the maximum economy of motion in all processes involving manual labor

The minor stoppages in the automated processes of the assembly line were partly caused by parts-handling problems, but the main problem was the excess time required for making adjustments in electronic circuits composed of semiconductors. Accordingly, it became apparent that reducing the minor stoppages in the assembly line depended upon greatly improving the quality of related upstream processes. A nine-month project to eliminate slight defects brought the following impressive results:

MTBF-min = 21 times greater
MTBF-cyc = 23 times greater
MTBF-cyc level after improvement: 10,000 cycles/process
Operator work efficiency (for entire line): 2.2 times greater

As a result, the improvement team achieved its goal of doubling productivity for the second consecutive year (see Figure 3-3).

SUCCESS WITH STAND-ALONE EQUIPMENT

At company C, a device called an electronic part inserter functions to automatically insert and fasten electronic components that have protruding leads (such as capacitors, resistors,

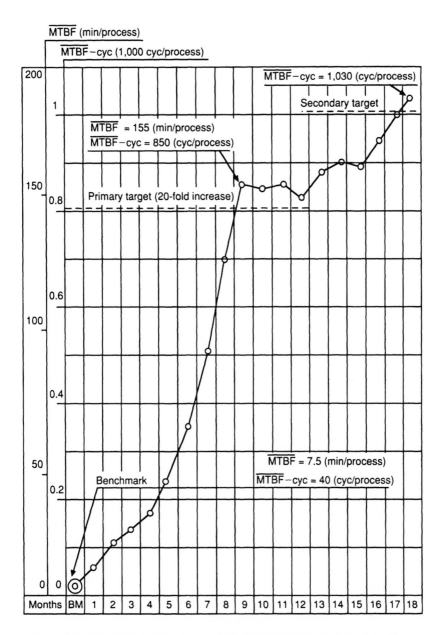

Figure 3-3. Results of Improvement Project (Average Values for 40 Processes in Automated Assembly Line)

and coils) onto printed circuit boards. This is accomplished by having several dozen types of parts taped in a row as shown in Figure 3-4. These rows of parts are supplied to a sequencer that arranges them into a *sequential tape* in which each component is set in the order of its insertion, as shown in Figure 3-5. The inserter receives programmed instructions for automatically inserting, fastening, and inspecting hundreds of components onto each printed circuit board, as shown in Figures 3-6 and 3-7.

The inserter is especially prone to operational errors; to insert a single component, it must execute six complicated motions within 0.2 to 0.4 seconds. Furthermore, it must treat the tape and leads very gently while remaining extremely sensitive to the precision requirements of the component insertion holes on the printed circuit board.

Although designed as a fully automatic piece of equipment, the inserter required such frequent attention because of error-caused stoppages that the human workers dared not leave it running unsupervised (for example, during the lunch hour). The improvement team's activities eventually expanded to include the elimination of slight defects in the sequencer and

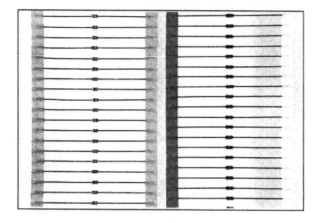

Figure 3-4. Taped Components

inserter, improvement of printed circuit board processing, and program improvements. The results of these efforts are shown in Figure 3-8.

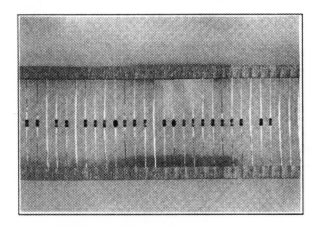

Figure 3-5. Sequentially Taped Components

Figure 3-6. Printed Circuit Board

Figure 3-7. Inserter

The results are summarized as follows:

MTBF-min: 24 times greater
MTBF-cyc: 24 times greater
MTBF-cyc level after improvement: 20,000 cycles/process
UR-2: 1.5 times greater
Operator work efficiency: 3.0 times greater

As a result, minor stoppages were reduced to $1/24$ of their previous level and the workers were able to let the inserter operate automatically during the lunch hour.

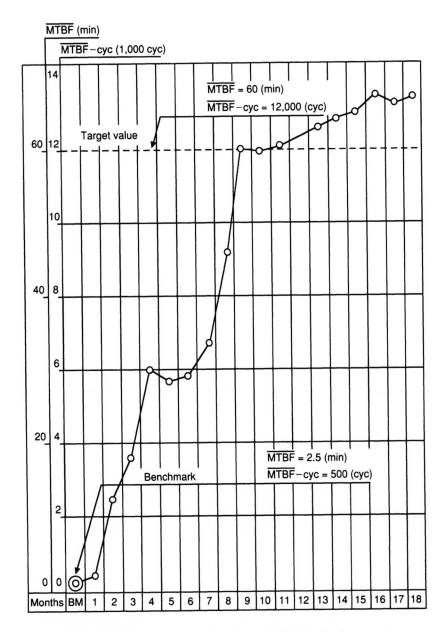

Figure 3-8. Results of Improvement Project (Electronic Component Inserter)

4

The Need for Improvement

It is hardly necessary to explain the need for a reduction in the number of minor stoppages. After all, anyone who works at or with production lines — from operators, technical staff, and process planners to managers concerned with investment planning or equipment operations — has been bothered by minor stoppages enough to keenly appreciate the need for improvements designed to eliminate them.

Unfortunately, all too often, daily recognition of the need for these improvements is nothing more than wishful thinking. Some people have even given up hope of improvement, figuring that minor stoppages are inevitable in machines that are as automated, rapid, and complex as the ones they are using. Other people can clearly see the need for improvements, but they are uncertain about what can actually be done.

Improvement plans work if they are properly implemented. However, one of the greatest obstacles to improvement is the attitude that, since most minor stoppages can be quickly dealt with by manual resetting, it is OK *for the time being* to have people react to them rather than work to make preventive improvements.

So, what people need to recognize is not so much the need for improvements as the need to become adamant and confident in making such improvements. As will be explained in Chapter 5, many minor stoppages are linked to slight defects, and eliminating such defects requires tenacious and ongoing improvement efforts. The case studies described in this book attest to this fact. Once people recognize that it is indeed possible to make improvements, they can put their wishful thinking to good use in carrying them out.

People can handle it for the time being.

FACTORS THAT CONTRIBUTE TO AN INCREASE IN MINOR STOPPAGES

Two factors have led to an increase in the frequency of minor stoppages: the trend toward automation and the trend toward linked processes. Each of these factors is examined in the following sections.

The Trend Toward Automation

This book deals exclusively with minor stoppages that occur in automated equipment. Minor stoppages were not much of a problem in older and simpler versions of today's automated equipment. These were generally stand-alone units in which only the *processing* parts were actually automated. Even in equipment that also featured automatic loading of materials, these materials were usually continuously connected items such as wire or hoops, and processed goods were simply unloaded into chutes through which they fell, into a heap, in some kind of container. However, in much of today's automated equipment, parts must be loaded and unloaded in discrete units, so minor stoppages become a major problem.

Besides this, automated assembly is usually done at high speed, which makes minor stoppages an even greater problem. Automated assembly presents three problems in terms of minor stoppages.

1. It requires high precision in parts handling.
2. It requires the handling of parts that have various shapes and sizes.
3. Any quality problems that exist in discrete parts or in subassembled parts will get carried into the assembly process.

The faster a machine operates, the more likely it is to experience errors. The trend in both automatic processing and automatic assembly is toward higher speeds, which means more minor stoppages.

In addition, minor stoppages are much more common during parts handling processes when the parts are oddly shaped, or very small, very soft, or very light.

Automated lines combine the trend toward automated equipment with the trend toward linked processes, and this combination naturally produces lots of minor stoppages. In advanced factories, more than 20 automated machines can be directly linked with no stock between them. The overall reliability rate of such a line is the product of all the reliability rates for each individual machine. In other words, if any one of the processes in the line has a low reliability rate, the line is likely to experience a minor stoppage every few seconds.

Often, a company that has a high level of production technology at one of its factories, and already spends a lot of time fixing minor stoppages there, will decide to introduce similar high-level automation at its other factories. As a result, the company discovers that minor stoppages continue to make things difficult, even for the new, supposedly *automated* operations.

The Trend Toward Linked Processes

Linking processes is being promoted as a means of greatly reducing production lead time, and also reducing between-process stock and between-process handling loss. Naturally, when a line consists of directly linked processes with no stock between them, a stoppage at any of the processes means the whole line must stop.

If n represents the number of processes in a linked line, we can say that the loss incurred by a stoppage at one process becomes multiplied by a factor of n. It thus becomes quite clear

Linked processes

why the trend toward linked processes has made minor stoppages a much more serious problem.

THE EFFECTS OF MINOR STOPPAGES

The losses incurred by minor stoppages affect the three key
production factors of quality, cost, and delivery (QCD).
Sometimes safety problems are also created. The need for
improvements obviously stems from these types of losses, but it
is important for people to understand that these losses are
avoidable.

Automated Equipment and Automated Lines

Automated equipment and automated lines are generally
the result of long years of research and large-scale investment.
The whole point of them is to substantially improve productivity.
Minor stoppages, though apparently trifling little things, can
keep higher productivity vexingly beyond reach for the following reasons.

1. A new piece of automated equipment or an automated
   line cannot be operated using the specified number of
   people, so some extra staff must be assigned. In many
   cases, companies have found that they need to assign
   about twice as many people to the line as they had
   expected.
2. The effective capacity utilization rate for the equipment
   does not rise. It is not unusual for minor stoppages to
   result in direct equipment efficiency loss of from 20 to
   30 percent.
3. Although the equipment unit or line is supposed to be
   fully automatic, the factory workers find that they cannot let it operate unattended, and this results in many
   lost opportunities for higher capacity utilization.
4. The losses mentioned in 2 and 3, preceding, mean that

the company must build two automated lines to produce the output they had thought possible from just one line. Of course, having two lines means the company is suffering twice as much loss.

Line Using Human Operators and Robots or Automated Equipment

In some assembly lines, such as those required for complex products, the line consists of several dozen processes, some of which involve manual work, while the rest are handled automatically by robots or other automated equipment. The minor stoppages that are due to operational errors in the automated equipment are a major hindrance to the productivity of the many human workers. This is because they must adapt to frequent line stops, each of which interrupts the pace of their operations and breaks their work rhythms. This leads to greater fatigue among workers. In addition, human assistance is needed to fix problems at the automated processes.

Automated Process Directly Linked to Manual Production Line

This is the type of situation in which an automated process is directly linked to a general assembly line composed entirely of manual operations, or a situation in which a manual line is directly linked to an automated process such as a packaging machine. Here too, minor stoppages at the automated process can have a severe impact on the manual production line. This type of problem has already been described.

Pay particular attention, however, to lines in which relatively few of the minor stoppages are actually remedied by human intervention. This is usually indicative of an effort to prevent these stoppages from lowering the productivity of the entire line.

Obstacles to Further Automation

When minor stoppages become too frequent, there are no advantages to linking automated processes (that is, combining automation with linked processes).

In many cases, a preponderance of minor stoppages in the main operation of the line (such as automated assembly) makes it impossible to automate related equipment such as conveyance systems.

The Safety Standpoint

Because fixing minor stoppages often means manually repairing and adjusting equipment that is in operation, it makes sense from the safety standpoint to have as few stoppages as possible.

Fixing a minor stoppage can be dangerous.

5

An Approach to
Finding Solutions

UNDERSTANDING MINOR STOPPAGE PHENOMENA

Minor stoppages tend to occur quite frequently; however, a steady stream of them does not necessarily indicate that errors are occurring whenever the equipment operates. Neither does it mean that the equipment is producing nothing but defective goods, for if this was the case, then every equipment operation would contain an error, and the entire process would be inoperable. The occurrence of minor stoppages indicates that the equipment is generally running well but that a certain number of errors occur in its operation. This seemingly simple point is crucial to an understanding of minor stoppage phenomena and to finding solutions to the problems they cause.

This point can be examined from a quantitative perspective. Consider, for example, a stand-alone process in which the MTBF-min is approximately three minutes. This means that someone has to lend a hand to fix a minor stoppage at this process about 160 times during an eight-hour shift. This is typical for automated processes that have a rapid cycle time ranging from 0.2 to 4.0 seconds.

If the cycle time is 0.3 seconds with an MTBF-min of 3 minutes (180 seconds), then the MTBF-cyc is 600 cycles. This means that, on the average, a minor stoppage will occur at this process once every 600 cycles. Although this process does suffer from minor stoppages, it is far from being an error-ridden process since errors occur only once every 600 cycles and the process operates normally in 998 of every 1,000 cycles.

Even if the cycle time is as high as four seconds and the MTBF-min remains at three minutes, there is still a rather low percentage of errors because, in this case, the MTBF-cyc is 45 cycles. This means that only about 2 percent of operations have errors, while 98 percent are error-free.

Looking at the situation from this perspective, you can see that even when equipment has minor stoppages, its overall condition is not error-prone enough to be thought of as abnormal. Instead, it has a tendency toward occasional changes that produce errors in some part of the equipment operations as a result of some combination of causes.

Causes as Combinations of Slight Defects

Consider an example of a typical parts feeder that channels and feeds transistors through a vibrating chute to an automated assembly line (see Figure 5-1). Minor stoppages occur when the transistors fail to feed properly, and this situation must be remedied by human intervention. These transistors are all of the same type, and although there may be a few defective ones, there are not enough to account for the frequency of minor stoppages at the feeder. An inspection of the feeder reveals only that it is clean and lubricated according to standards.

The only possible explanation for the minor stoppages is that the causes are related to slight deviations from the normal conditions. In other words, about once every three minutes (on the average) the conditions of the parts, workpieces, lubricant, or other elements vary enough that their combined influence on the equipment operation is enough to produce a minor stoppage.

This means that blame for the stoppages cannot be placed on any particular aspect of the parts feeder, but must instead be looked for in a combination of causes.

Figure 5-1. Parts Feeder

Looking for Slight Defects

A close study of the phenomena described in the following sections will help clarify the fluctuations and factors that cause occasional errors.

Slight Gap in Chute Connection

As can be seen in Figure 5-2, there is a slight gap in the connection between the upper and lower segments of the chute. This gap is not large enough to clog up the flow of transistors; if it were, the feeder would not operate at all, and that would not be a minor stoppage. Rather, the gap is no thicker than a single sheet of paper.

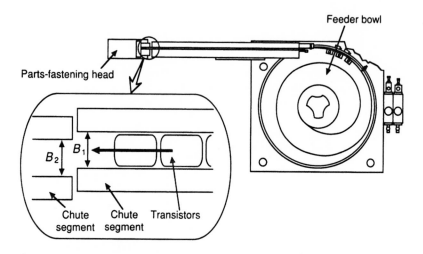

Figure 5-2. Slight Gap at Chute Connection

Small Burrs on Transistors

Some of the transistors have received small burrs on their molded casing. Most burrs are tiny, and all are within the tolerance range stipulated in quality specifications (see Figures 5-3 and 5-4).

Figure 5-3. Transistor

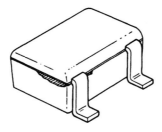

Figure 5-4. Small Burr on Transistor

Relation Between Slight Gap and Small Burrs

The two problems just described — the gap in the chute connection and the burrs on some transistors — create almost no errors (about 998 of every 1,000 parts are error-free). However, the size of the transistor burrs varies. Sometimes, transistors with relatively large burrs get caught on the gap in the chute connection, and this creates a conveyance error — in other words, a minor stoppage (see Figure 5-5).

Is the Chute Vibration Too Weak?

As a possible solution, the chute vibration was increased. This proved helpful to some extent in preventing the phenomenon of transistors getting caught at the chute connection point; however, the stronger vibration caused another type of problem. This new problem made it clear that the phenomenon could not be explained simply by the relationship between chute vibration rate and resistance caused by burrs on the transistor casings.

How Transistors Get Caught

The slight gap, the small burrs, and the vibration rate used to propel the transistors down the chute all combine to create this phenomenon. Since the mechanism behind this problem is caused by all three factors, simply increasing the vibration rate of the feeder is not a solution.

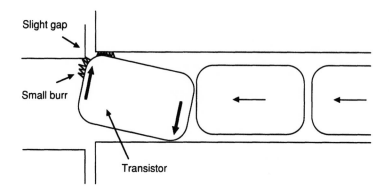

Slight gap

Small burr

Transistor

Figure 5-5. Burred Transistor Caught on Gap

This example shows how important it is to recognize when the mechanism behind a minor stoppage is actually a combination of slight defects.

Problems can be caused by a combination of slight defects.

Definition of Slight Defects

The preceding example described some slight defects in a parts feeding process. The term *slight defects* was coined by Dr. Masakatsu Nakaigawa, the creator of skills management, and it is a fundamental concept in the technical field of skills management.

Dr. Nakaigawa has offered the following description of slight defects.

- Slight defects are usually not even noticed, or if they are noticed, people tend to regard them as insignificant.
- Slight defects do not independently cause particular problems, but their synergistic or mutual effect can be enough to greatly harm productivity.
- In the book *Shinraisei kanri benran* (Reliability management handbook), Mr. R. Lusser discusses the fundamentals of reliability engineering, and argues that, based on the principle of multiplication, slight defects can work together to keep productivity levels down.

Lusser's Rule of Multiplication

The following paragraph is an excerpt from *Reliability Management Handbook*.

During World War II, Dr. Werner Von Braun led a group of scientists and engineers in the development of Germany's V1 rocket. Early on, they realized that breakdowns were the weakest link in the configuration of their rocket system. Wishing to overcome this weakness, Dr. E. Pieruschka, one of the group's members, asked fellow member Lusser to work on the problem. Lusser came up with his rule of multiplication, which states that every component has an effect on the system's reliability and that we can determine the system's reliability rate by multiplying the reliability rates of the components. This approach helped them design high reliability into each component, resulting in the development of the world's first rocket system, which had an impressive reliability rate of 75%.

APPROACH TO SOLVING MINOR STOPPAGE PROBLEMS

Slight Defects as Causes of Minor Stoppages

If any process has a 100 percent error rate for each of its operations, then obviously the basic conditions enabling the process to operate have not been established. However, processes that experience only a small percentage of errors indicate a lack of reliability that can usually best be addressed by considering slight defects to be the source of the problem.

This does not mean that slight defects are *behind* the causes of the problem: they *are* the causes. Recognition of this fact is the key to success in making improvements. However, even when people have a theoretical understanding of this approach to slight defects, they tend to have trouble putting it into practice when faced with troublesome equipment. You must be thoroughly determined to overcome this tendency and to get at the root of the problem — which means the slight defects — by tracing the causes and by learning from the case studies provided in this book.

Slight Defects as Initial Defects

When a newly installed piece of equipment has very few minor stoppages but then gradually experiences more and more, people tend to think that most of the slight defects causing the stoppages are the result of inadequate maintenance. However, such cases are actually very rare. In most cases, the newly installed equipment is not in very good shape to begin with and, after many adjustments, it works well enough so that its problems are limited to frequent minor stoppages. In other words, the equipment has always contained various slight defects (as initial defects), and these must be recognized as the causes of the ongoing minor stoppages. In such cases, making improvements is a lot like debugging defective systems.

Records show that more than 85 percent of the slight defects that have been addressed by minor stoppage improvement efforts are initial defects. This means that, for the most part, these improvement activities must venture into uncharted territory.

Part 2

The Improvement Program

6

Overview of
Improvement Steps

When making improvements to reduce the frequency of minor stoppages, be sure to observe the following key points.

- Make a new study of the structure, mechanisms, and operational principles of the target equipment.
- Do a cleaning inspection on all related equipment parts.
- Carefully observe the minor stoppage phenomena.
- Look at causes as mechanisms (or as hypotheses).
- Verify causal mechanisms.
- Establish improvement policies.
- Repeat the plan-do-check cycle in actual improvement measures.

BASIC STEPS

Figure 6-1 shows the eight basic steps in making minor stoppage improvements.

These steps, which are still being revised, are briefly described in the following text.

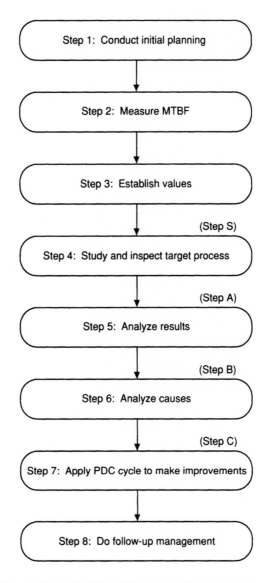

Figure 6-1. Basic Steps for Minor Stoppage Improvements

Step 1: Conduct Initial Planning

After establishing the general improvement goal for a particular automated machine or line, define the improvement theme and organize an improvement team.

Step 2: Measure MTBF

Check related standards and gather the necessary equipment for measuring the minor stoppage MTBF.

Step 3: Establish Values

Establish the benchmark value to indicate the *before improvement* level, and set the final target value. Divide the improvement process into monthly increments.

Step 4: Study and Inspect Target Process (Step S)

To track down causes and draft improvement plans accurately, first acquire a firm technical understanding of the target process and the equipment by studying them and doing cleaning inspections.

Step 5: Analyze Results (Step A)

As a prerequisite for an accurate investigation of causes, carefully observe and analyze minor stoppage phenomena from various perspectives.

Step 6: Analyze Causes (Step B)

To draft an effective improvement plan, identify the slight defects that cause the minor stoppages.

Step 7: Apply PDC Cycle to Make Improvements (Step C)

After identifying all of the slight defects that cause minor stoppages, diligently apply the PDC (plan-do-check) cycle in improvements designed to remove these defects and reach the target values.

Step 8: Do Follow-up Management

After the target values have been reached and the improvement theme has been completed, standardize the improvement and check results to ensure that improved conditions are maintained.

Steps 4, 5, 6, and 7 are also referred to as steps S, A, B, and C, respectively. Step 4, or step S (which stands for *study*), involves the important activity of studying and inspecting the target process and the equipment. Steps 5, 6, and 7 are the most important improvement activities, and they are repeated many times as the program progresses. The letters *A*, *B*, and *C* not only define the proper sequence for the steps but also stand for *analysis, breakdown*, and *create*.

SUBSTEPS

Figure 6-2 shows the breakdown of the 8 basic improvement steps into 18 substeps.

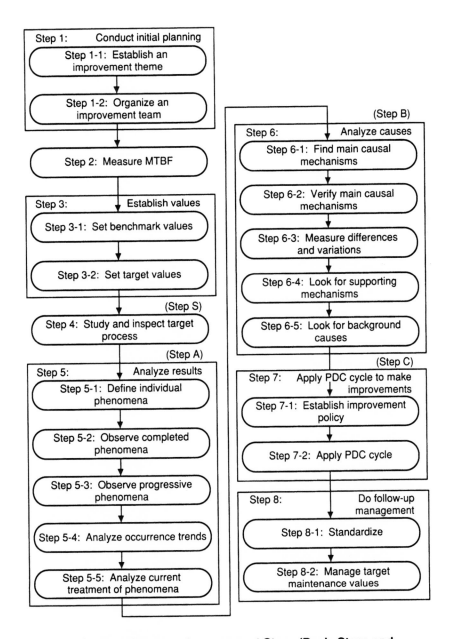

Figure 6-2. Minor Stoppage Improvement Steps (Basic Steps and Substeps)

7

Step 1:

Conduct Initial Planning

STEP 1-1: ESTABLISH AN IMPROVEMENT THEME

When someone notices frequent minor stoppages at a particular automated machine or automated line, he or she should submit a proposal describing the problem and the need for improvement. Then the problem can officially be taken up as an improvement theme for the company division or for the entire factory. Operators and other workers on the factory floor are seldom able to single-handedly tackle the kind of minor stoppage improvement problems required for today's sophisticated automated equipment, so improvement themes should be addressed at the departmental or factory level.

Some additional points should also be considered.

Be Thorough and Specific

Improvement plans are not supposed to be broad campaigns aimed at reducing minor stoppages throughout the entire factory. Rather, they should address particular minor stoppage problems at specific automated machines or automated lines. The best improvement results come from narrowly defined improvement efforts in which the team members concentrate on making thorough improvements in response to specific problems.

Choose Rewarding Problems, Not Easy Ones

When establishing improvement themes, try to select problems that can be clearly defined and that, if solved, promise significant benefits. If the theme is recognized as an important one, the improvement team will be less tempted to give up when difficulties arise. The team should be encouraged to seek help, whenever necessary, from people in other departments and to *persevere* until they achieve the improvement target.

Set Sufficiently High Goals

Before beginning any improvement project, answer the following two questions.

1. What are the specific reasons for making the improvement (reducing or eliminating the targeted minor stoppage)?
2. What kind of results can be expected if the improvement program is successful?

Most improvement projects run into difficulties, but these are easier to overcome if all members of the improvement team have a common understanding of what they are trying to achieve and why. This is an important point. You must decide on a case-by-case basis what you expect to achieve with each minor stoppage improvement.

A list of some goals that have been pursued in actual improvement projects follows.

- Reduce the number of operators on an automated line.
- Increase the number of automated machines.

Sufficiently high goals

- Ensure reliable automatic operation during breaks and off-hours.
- Increase the time-based output (the effective capacity utilization rate of the equipment).
- Establish links between automated equipment units in an automated line to increase productivity.
- Reduce the number of defective products (that is, raise the nondefective yield).

STEP 1-2: ORGANIZE AN IMPROVEMENT TEAM

The improvement effort should be made by a team consisting primarily of people whose work is directly related to the problem at hand. Most minor stoppage improvement themes are aimed at long-neglected, initial, slight defects in the target equipment; therefore, the improvement group should almost always include at least one technician from the department using the equipment, or one PM (preventive maintenance) specialist from the manufacturing division. Most improvement themes also concern quality problems, which means that the team should also include a quality manager.

Minor stoppages usually involve precision factors such as process changeover settings and operating condition settings, a full knowledge of which is generally beyond the expertise of any one individual. Therefore, these problems are rarely solved single-handedly by the person responsible for the equipment, by the PM specialist, or by the quality manager.

Another reason why improvements should be made by teams is that the PM activities that are used to routinely inspect the equipment and discover abnormalities require the participation of factory-floor workers (equipment operators). It is also the factory-floor people who are chiefly responsible for checking on the supply of parts, verifying the quality of assembled goods, and performing other quality-checking tasks. Unless the team includes the operators who will be responsible for enforcing the correct procedures, it will be difficult indeed for any equipment technician or quality improvement specialist to make successful improvements.

Thus, it is essential that the improvement team be composed of people from various ranks in the factory organization, including the section chief and others who are involved in the related production activities and are responsible for the production equipment. This constellation of team members should also include specialists from the production engineering, equipment, and quality control departments.

Although there is no need to directly involve higher-ups such as the manufacturing division chief or the factory superintendent, their acknowledgment and support of improvement projects is also a key ingredient for success.

Active Members and Supporting Members

Generally, improvement teams are organized so that they are made up of both active members and supporting members.

Active members usually include the relevant manufacturing section chief and his or her subordinates, while supporting members usually include engineers, equipment technicians, and clerical staff. After much experimentation, it has been determined that this type of team organization works best to promote improvements if each team member has clearly defined responsibilities.

Figure 7-1 shows an example of this type of improvement promotion organization. It is suitable not only for minor stoppage improvements, but also for various other types of improvements that aim to increase the effective capacity utilization of automated equipment, or that aim to reduce quality defects.

At factory T belonging to company A, the manufacturing chief came up with the motto "Together, we can do it" for all the slight defect improvement activities at the factory. The shortest and surest road to success lies in concentrated and well-organized improvement activities.

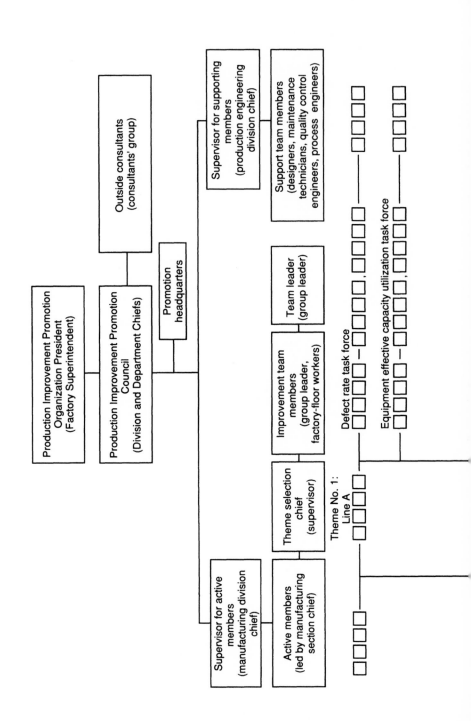

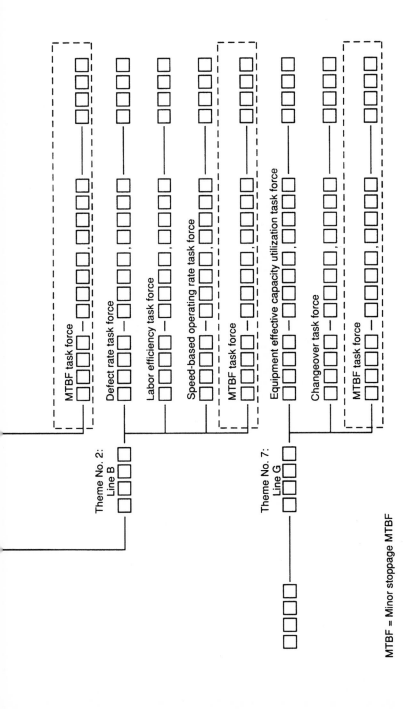

MTBF = Minor stoppage MTBF

Figure 7-1. Example of Improvement Promotion Organization

8

Step 2:

Measure MTBF

OUTPUT DATA

Throughout the improvement program, the MTBF should be continually measured until it reaches the target value. An example of MTBF recordkeeping is described in the following text.

Monthly MTBF Statistics

Keeping track of monthly MTBF statistics allows workers to see the progress being made toward the improvement goal. Graphs, such as the one shown in Figure 8-1, make these result statistics easy to understand.

Pareto Analysis of Monthly Minor Stoppage Statistics

Keep in mind the key improvement points while making improvements. Make preparatory studies of the minor stoppages and sort out the various types of minor stoppage phenomena.

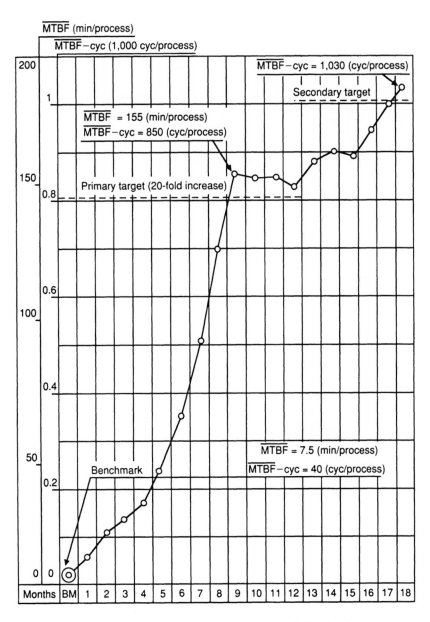

Figure 8-1. Minor Stoppage Improvement Result Statistics for Automated Assembly Line (Average Value for Line Composed of 40 Processes)

When working with automated lines made up of several machines, start by studying the machine-specific phenomena, which you can then list as categories on Pareto diagrams such as the one shown in Figure 8-2. In this figure, the Pareto diagram shows several categories of phenomena for a minor stoppage that occurs at a single equipment unit.

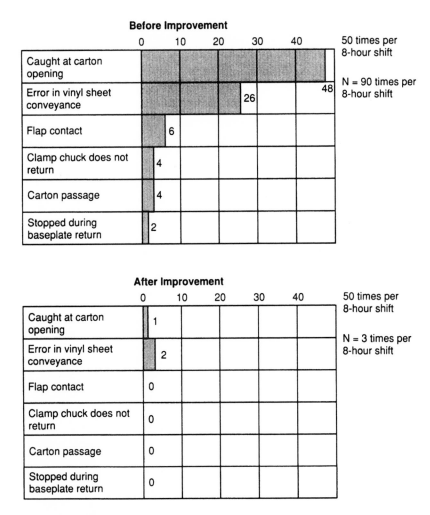

Figure 8-2. Example of Pareto Analysis

When only one or two of the categories of phenomena account for the vast majority of minor stoppages, you can make a secondary Pareto diagram to break down each of those categories into more detailed subcategories.

Daily MTBF Statistics

Daily (or per-shift) MTBF statistics can also be taken and charted. The analysis of occurrence frequency, described later on, can provide very useful data showing which improvement measures are the most effective. When compiling such daily statistics, record the number of stoppage occurrences for the three most important phenomena.

INPUT DATA

Nf Data (Number of Minor Stoppages)

As mentioned earlier, manually recording the number of minor stoppages usually results in inaccuracies. Because continual MTBF measurement depends on a reliable counting method, replace manual recording with a mechanical counter.

Besides making preparatory studies of minor stoppages and categorizing minor stoppage phenomena, also make policy decisions on the following questions.

- How are the processes to be divided for counting purposes?
- What kind of stoppages happen that are not actually error related? Can they be distinguished from other stoppages and mechanically counted?

At the very least, use counters to keep a continual and accurate count of the overall number of minor stoppages. Ideally, use separate automatic counters for each type of minor stoppage phenomena; however, this may prove too costly.

OT (Operating Time) Data

Using a mechanical counter is certainly the most reliable means of recording the number of minor stoppages. However, measuring the effective capacity utilization rate of the equipment is another useful method. To calculate it, you need data concerning the time-based capacity utilization rate of the equipment, and this can be acquired through the use of mechanical recorders.

If the operation time is based on the ACT (actual cycle time), establish a method for obtaining the raw data for the ACT and the actual number of work hours (Nk).

DATA CALCULATIONS

The calculations for these data were described in Chapter 2. This section briefly covers the calculation of Nf (number of minor stoppages). If the counter records stoppages that do not qualify as minor stoppages, find a formula by which to identify and subtract the unrelated stops.

Frequency Factors

Frequency factors such as stoppages for routine changeover, feeding in materials, removing processed goods, and routine quality checks are not errors and should not be counted as such. However, stoppages that are made for retooling and quality checks in response to particular problems rather than as part of routine maintenance should be included as minor stoppages (caused by errors).

Other Stoppages

Changeover for new models (as required in the production schedule) and rest stops for equipment that is not supposed to operate automatically during rest periods or before and after work shifts, are not to be regarded as error-caused stops. If the stop counter cannot avoid counting these stops, you must either revert to manual stop counting or find some average figure that represents such non-error stops and that can be subtracted from the total number shown on the counter.

9

Step 3:
Establish Values

STEP 3-1: SET BENCHMARK VALUES

Benchmark values are the *before improvement values* that are determined by measuring conditions at the start of improvement activities. In minor stoppage improvement projects, use the target equipment (or line) minor stoppage MTBF as the benchmark value. Obviously, unless you start out with this value, you cannot judge how much progress has been made during the improvement activities.

Anticipated Minor Stoppages

Sometimes, an operator who is in the right place at the right time can notice when a part gets stuck in a chute and can then fix the problem before it causes a minor stoppage. This method of preventing stoppages is costly because it requires extra labor. However, it is important to be aware of cases like this because, even though a minor stoppage did not actually occur, the causes (conditions) are still present, and there is need for improvement. These manually prevented problems are called *anticipated minor stoppages*. Since they cannot be counted under normal operating conditions, it is difficult to keep track of them, so make a special effort to find them and be sure they are counted.

Specifically, take one of the following measures:

1. Instruct the operators not to fix problems that they recognize as leading to minor stoppages, so that the stoppages will actually occur and be counted, or
2. Instruct the operators to continue fixing problems that they recognize as leading to minor stoppages, but require them to record each incident. The use of video cameras is one way of recording such events over a period of several hours.

There have been some cases in which carrying out such special efforts and keeping track of anticipated minor stoppages has raised the total count by as much as 60 percent.

STEP 3-2: SET TARGET VALUES

When target values are set too low, improvement projects tend to proceed smoothly and successfully, but their results are worth little. Such improvements are not likely to free the equipment operators from the vicious cycle of troubleshooting. Conversely, when target values are set high, the road to success may be full of difficulties. Overcoming these difficulties, however, is often the key to discovering the technical mechanisms behind the causes of minor stoppages and to developing management techniques that forestall occurrence of such problems. Thus, the question is, how do you know which target value is high enough without being impossibly high?

It is not easy to establish a concrete guideline for setting target levels. To do it right, you need extensive experience in improvement projects as well as a certain amount of courage in deciding where to draw the line. Dr. Masakatsu Nakaigawa has recommended 0.1 percent or less as a concrete target value for the process defect rate within the context of skills management. This is a good, challenging target level.

Dr. Shigeo Shingo, another leading quality control consultant, recommends 10 minutes as the absolute maximum time to be allowed for single changeovers. His guidelines, based on much firsthand experience, have had an enormous and concrete impact.

Simple and clear-cut target values may complicate improvement efforts, but the rewards of success are well worth it.

Minor Stoppage Target Values

The MTBF target values recommended in this book are based on my own experience with minor stoppage improvement efforts centering on automated assembly equipment and automated lines. A good rule of thumb is this: Reduce quality problems to $1/10$ or less of their previous level, and reduce the frequency of minor stoppages to at least $1/20$ of its previous level (that is, increase the MTBF 20-fold). Merely halving the number of minor stoppages does not produce dramatic improvement and is not worth the effort.

Relative Target: 20-fold or Greater Increase in MTBF

This is the minimum target that improvement teams should pursue when they are troubled by frequent minor stoppages and want to do something about it. They can use the following absolute target as a guideline to help determine whether such a 20-fold increase is possible.

Absolute Target:

MTBF-cyc = at least 10,000 (cycles/process)
This absolute target formula is a good guideline for check-

ing the degree of operational reliability of equipment that automatically handles individual parts. For such equipment, the absolute target $\overline{\text{MTBF}}$-cyc value of 10,000 (cycles/process) corresponds to a reliability rating of 99.99 percent (.01 percent error).

For equipment such as high-speed automated presses that use continuous-feed materials such as hoops or wires, the absolute target $\overline{\text{MTBF}}$-cyc value ranges from 100,000 to 1,000,000 cycles/process.

The number of individual processes must conform to the organization chart established by the production engineering division of the factory. In many cases, each process consists of a single unit of equipment. However, some factories have processing or assembly stations, each made up of several equipment units; and in this case each process consists of a single station. Figure 9-1 shows the MTBF-min values for a stand-alone process having an MTBF-cyc measurement of 10,000 cycles.

Cycle time (seconds)	MTBF-min (minutes)
0.3	50
4	600
12	2,000
20	3,000
30	5,000
40	6,000
60	10,000

Figure 9-1. MTBF-min Values for Stand-alone Process where MTBF−cyc= 10,000 Cycles

Examples of Target Values

Getting equipment to operate automatically during the lunch hour. It is alarmingly common for so-called automated processes to have a minor stoppage MTBF of 2 or 3 minutes, so that manual assistance is needed from 100 to 200 times every 8-hour shift.

Most of these processes have rapid cycle times ranging from 0.2 to 4.0 seconds, and since the equipment is often brand new, such problems are serious obstacles to productivity. As was mentioned in Chapter 2, when a factory manager gives a figure of 2 or 3 minutes as a rough approximation of the average MTBF for a process, it is not unusual that careful measurement of the actual MTBF shows a much worse figure. So, many factories are faced with the irony that their supposedly fully automatic process equipment cannot be left to operate automatically during the lunch hour or other off-duty hours.

Improvement projects have demonstrated that improvement teams can achieve the relative target of a 20-fold increase in the MTBF, thereby increasing the reliability of their automated equipment to the point where it can be left to operate alone during the off-duty hours.

Figure 9-2 gives a comparison of minor stoppage MTBF values of 3 minutes and 60 minutes (20 times greater) for 2 process lines having different cycle times.

Increasing the minor stoppage MTBF to once every shift. If the minor stoppage MTBF is currently every 20 to 30 minutes, a 20-fold increase would mean an MTBF of about once every 8-hour shift. Obviously, such MTBF figures can apply only to a process for which the cycle time is rather long (at least 20 seconds).

Let us see how a target MTBF value of once every shift might be calculated in the case of an automated line consisting of four or five processes. Each process has a cycle time of about 12 seconds, and the line has an output of about 2,000 units every

Cycle time		0.25 seconds	4 seconds
Process line		Linked inserters (No. of processes = 2)	Automated assembly line (No. of processes = 6)
Output per shift		100,000 units	6,000 units
No. of cycles per process per minor stoppage	MTBF = approx. 3 minutes	1,500 cycles	300 cycles
	MTBF = approx. 60 minutes	30,000 cycles	6,000 cycles

Figure 9-2. MTBF Values for Two Process Lines

eight-hour shift. Calculate the $\overline{\text{MTBF}}$-cyc value for such a line by determining the number of cycles for that line during one shift, as follows.

> 2,000 cycles (cycles per shift per process) × 4 or 5 (processes) = 8,000 to 10,000 (cycles per shift)

One minor stoppage per shift gives an $\overline{\text{MTBF}}$-cyc value of 8,000 to 10,000, which is very close to the absolute target $\overline{\text{MTBF}}$-cyc value.

Setting Targets Based on High Objectives

It is not within the scope of this book to describe situations in which improvement teams have set target values that have proved impossible. Note, however, that it is easy to set target values based simply on high objectives. Improvement groups would be smart to use the methods just described to determine whether their target values are indeed feasible.

Dividing Up Monthly Target Values

How many months to reach the target? When it is not possible to establish a firm schedule and deadline for the improvement project, use the following guideline.

Suppose that a six-month schedule has been established for an improvement project that seeks to achieve a 20-fold increase in MTBF for a single automated machine or an automated line consisting of about 10 processes. To reduce minor stoppages to $1/20$ their previous level, you could reduce the current level by 50 percent a total of 4.3 times. However, past results indicate that breaking the schedule into 4.3 short-term goals has not been an effective strategy. Improvement projects at most factories have made faster progress when they pursue the single goal of reducing minor stoppages to $1/20$ their previous level within six months, even though this means setting a longer-term goal.

Splitting progress into monthly segments. If, by using the results of preparatory studies of minor stoppages, you can get an accurate reading of the items to be improved and the time needed to make the improvements, you can then establish a monthly timetable for achieving progress toward the target value. This is the best approach, and some improvement teams have been successful in following it. However, in most cases, it is very difficult to ascertain beforehand just what items will need to be improved and how long such improvements will take. In these cases, it is best to simply divide the targeted amount of improvement into equal monthly segments.

In the case of a program aimed at reducing minor stoppages to $1/20$ their previous level in six months, divide the amount of improvement needed into monthly segments that form a geometric progression toward the target value, as shown in Equation 15.

$$X^6 = 20 \implies 6 \log X = \log 20 \implies X \fallingdotseq 1.65$$

Equation 15

Figure 9-3 illustrates how these calculations can be translated as increased MTBF values on a line graph.

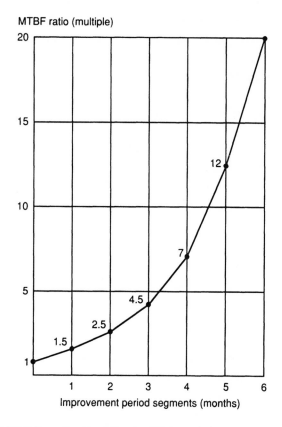

Figure 9-3. MTBF Ratio Increases as a Geometric Progression over a Six-month Period of Steady Progress in MTBF Improvement

Dividing Target Values into Major Phenomena Categories

A good way to organize the improvement program and chart its progress is to set separate improvement target values for each of the major improvement phenomena identified by Pareto analysis when the benchmark value was measured. This method also helps to clarify how the burden of improvement work is distributed.

Although a reduction in minor stoppages to $1/20$ the original level theoretically means a similar reduction in each of the related stoppage phenomena, consider the following:

- Some phenomena deserve more emphasis than others. The items that score higher on the Pareto charts will produce greater effects when improved.
- When broken down into categories of phenomena, some improvement targets are easier to achieve than others; some can be lowered to less than $1/20$ the previous level, while others cannot. The result is a mixed bag of improvement progress schedules that add up to the targeted amount of improvement.

10

Step 4:
Study and Inspect
Target Process (Step S)

At this step the essential part of minor stoppage improvement begins. This is also known as step S (for *study*).

The way to solve problems is to find out the *why* and *how* of things. When a metal damage specialist looks at a damaged piece of metal, he or she examines it from various perspectives to determine whether the damage was due to metal fatigue or defective material.

There is no point in beginning something you do not understand. Therefore, begin an improvement project by studying the engineering principles of the target process in order to accurately identify the causes of the problem; in other words, to find out *why* the problem occurs. This enables you to work out an improvement plan (the *how*) that makes successful improvement possible. Start by taking a fresh look at the target process.

The phenomena behind most minor stoppage problems are errors in parts handling; however, the person using sophisticated automated equipment does not necessarily understand everything about its mechanical structure and other details. Moreover, when parts get as small as a millimeter and operating speeds are on the order of milliseconds, there is little anyone can do to even directly (visually) check minor stoppage phenomena. If it is not possible to check something visually, it is necessary to make estimates. Making accurate estimates, however, requires knowledge of engineering principles.

The following is a general guide for improvement activities that deal with parts handling. It indicates what knowledge and methods are needed to make this kind of improvement.

TYPE OF INFORMATION REQUIRED

Here are some things that the active members of the improvement team need to know about the target process, and especially about the related equipment.

Structure of Direct Sections

Direct sections are sections of the process or equipment that come into direct contact with the parts, or that directly handle the parts. Leaving aside the question of whether the root causes of handling errors are actually located in these direct sections, it is nevertheless essential that the active team members understand the structure of these sections before attempting to make improvements. Although the equipment operators who daily fix minor stoppages in the equipment and the active team members who have already begun studying the equipment may both have some knowledge of the structure of these sections, such knowledge is not often complete, especially when the equipment is complex.

Operation of Direct Sections

The improvement team members must learn how each direct section relates to the parts being handled and to the purpose of the process.

Basic Operations and Detailed Operations

There is no need to devote much study to simple and *basic* operations such as the suction action of suction pads. However, if those suction pads had a device attached to the back of them that increased their suction force, it would be necessary to study and understand that type of *detailed* operation to identify all of the slight defects behind the minor stoppage problems.

Workings of Complicated Mechanisms

To understand the operations of direct sections that include complicated mechanisms, study:

- the operation steps of the direct section
- the purpose of each operation step
- how various direct sections contribute to each operation step

The supporting members (technical staff, and so on) must not only study the direct sections but should also become familiar with the detailed background mechanisms and control devices.

Necessary Conditions for Direct Sections

While it is the direct sections that actually achieve the purpose of the process, these sections have prerequisite conditions that are necessary for normal operations, and that can also be directly responsible for creating minor stoppages.

Static Conditions

The following are examples of static conditions for direct sections.

Chute connection. In a feeder chute made of two segments, no gap is allowed between the chute segments at the point where they abut. If any gap exists, parts can get hung up on it, as shown in Figure 10-1.

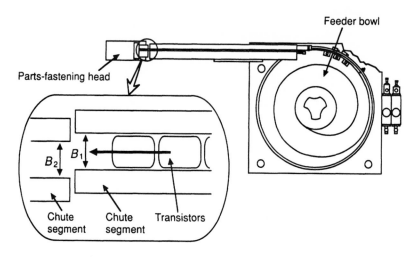

Figure 10-1. Slight Gap in Chute Connection

Suction cups. On a device that uses suction cups to lift parts, all cups must be aligned on the horizontal within a vertical range of plus or minus 1 millimeter. If the cups are out of alignment, some will be forced to carry too much weight and the part will fall, as shown in Figure 10-2.

Suction nozzle. If a suction device with a nozzle is used to manipulate parts, the nozzle tip must be cut at 90 degrees to the axis. If the tip is cut at any other angle, the part will tilt when picked up and will not be able to be set back down accurately (see Figure 10-3).

Reference surface for jig positioning. A part cannot be positioned correctly unless it is set precisely on the jig (see Figure 10-4).

Suction arm. There must be no looseness anywhere in a suction arm used to manipulate parts. Any looseness will cause

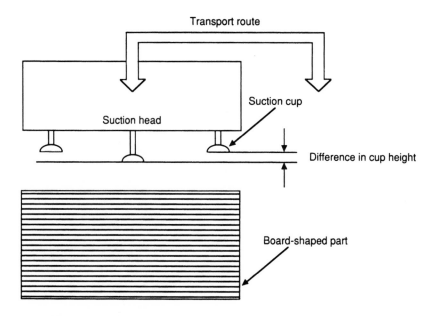

Figure 10-2. Suction Cups

the part being lifted to rub against the guide and fall, as shown in Figure 10-5.

Part positioning prongs. If a pair of mechanical prongs is used to center a part, it must do so to within 0.05 mm accuracy. If this standard is not met, the suction nozzle used to pick up the part will not be able to get a good hold on it, and the part may be dropped, as shown in Figure 10-6.

Dynamic Conditions for Direct Sections

The following are examples of dynamic conditions for direct sections.

Shock at end of suction arm stroke. The shock generated at the end of a suction arm stroke produces a force on the part. This force must be smaller than the gripping strength of the suction arm; otherwise, the part may slip from its correct position.

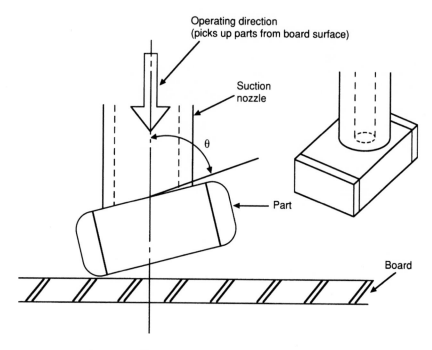

Figure 10-3. Suction Nozzle

Suction strength of suction nozzle. The suction strength of a nozzle must be increased to a certain level before the suction arm is raised; otherwise, the part may slip or may not be picked up at all.

Part detector pin speed. In order for a part to be lifted, the speed of the part detector pin must be increased to a value that prevents the part from dropping.

Chuck release timing. For the part to remain correctly positioned, it must not be released until after it has been set down.

Separation of part from suction cups. The part must be released from all suction cups simultaneously; otherwise, the part may slip and drop.

Timing of part extraction from magazine. The extraction motion must be synchronized with the timing of the motion of

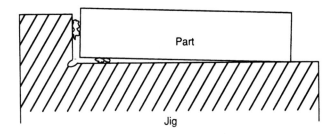

Figure 10-4. Reference Surface for Part Positioning in Jig

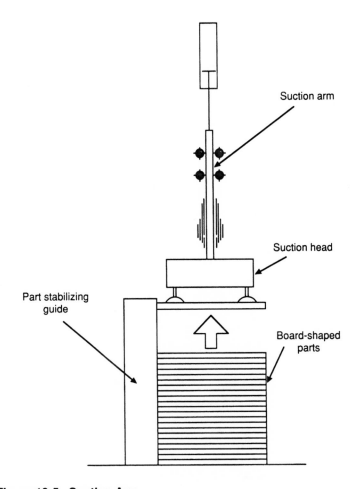

Figure 10-5. Suction Arm

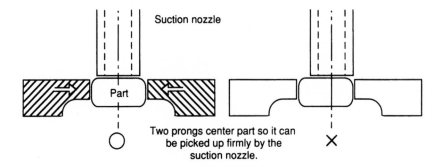

Figure 10-6. Part Positioning Prongs

the conveyor pocket; otherwise, the part will not be inserted into the conveyor pocket correctly.

SOURCES OF INFORMATION

Manuals

When the equipment comes with user manuals supplied by the manufacturer, the team members should study these manuals together to refresh their understanding of the equipment structure, operation, common operation errors, and other management points.

Drawings and Specifications

If there are no user manuals or if the manuals do not describe management points such as common operation errors, team members can still learn much from the equipment drawings and specifications. They should also study the quality standards and other standards for related materials and parts.

Guidance from Engineers

If the equipment was developed or modified in-house, the engineers involved are a good source of information. Additional guidance and support can often be obtained from engineers from outside manufacturers.

Discussion

The team members should think about and discuss the various conditions that are required for correct operation of the direct sections.

Cleaning Inspection

Cleaning inspections are a good way to learn about the structure of the equipment. When they perform a cleaning inspection on the functional parts of the equipment, team members notice defects that have always been overlooked. Typical examples of such defects include:

- loose screws or bolts in mechanisms
- dirt, dents and scrapes, abnormal abrasion, gaps, and other defects that interfere with the equipment operation
- looseness or vibration in mechanisms

Figure 10-7. Example of Target Equipment for Cleaning Inspection

- damaged gauges (for example, pressure gauges)
- worn or frayed electrical wiring
- dirty photoelectric tubes

Getting your hands on equipment during the cleaning process helps develop a more thorough understanding of the equipment than could be arrived at by theoretical knowledge alone. That is what is meant by the slogan *cleaning is where inspection begins*. And since the purpose of inspection is to discover abnormalities, *cleaning inspection* also serves as a step in discovering the causes of minor stoppages.

At this step, it is important that the direct sections be cleaned as thoroughly as possible, and that the team members learn about the equipment as they clean it. At step 6 (analyze causes), the team members conduct an overhaul inspection during which they disassemble, clean, and inspect the mechanisms.

11

Step 5:

Analyze Results (Step A)

Now that the observations and estimations are completed, it is time to begin an analysis of the facts. This step is also known as step A (for *analysis*). The procedure is similar to that followed by a detective at the scene of a crime — that is, checking for fingerprints and footprints, inspecting broken windows and other objects, and examining fragments left by the criminal. It can also be compared to the way in which a doctor investigates a disease — by checking the patient's blood pressure and examining X-ray images, brain waves, and so on.

This sort of analysis is a necessary part of the search for causes and the establishment of a treatment program.

For a minor stoppage improvement team, defining the theme of the improvement program often proves to be the most serious obstacle. The problem often lies in the difficulty of accurately identifying the actual causes of the minor stoppage, even when there are many possible causes from which to choose. Similarly, if a team is having a hard time establishing an effective strategy or action plan, it is usually because team members have an inadequate understanding of the causes.

Analyzing the facts

In both cases, there is simply not enough accurate information available to permit an informed decision. During their study of the available facts, team members should constantly be on the lookout for clues or new information that would help them more clearly define the causes. Unfortunately, it is easy to neglect this process. Improvement teams usually tend to shorten it to *find the facts and then plan the improvement*, or *find some possible causes and then plan the improvement*. However, it is best to do a proper analysis of both the facts and the causes before planning the improvement program. This analysis can be broken down into the following activities:

1. Define individual phenomena
2. Observe completed phenomena (target process or equipment after a minor stoppage has occurred)
3. Observe progressive phenomena
4. Analyze occurrence trends
5. Analyze current treatment of phenomena.

STEP 5-1: DEFINE INDIVIDUAL PHENOMENA

The individual minor stoppage phenomena that become targets for improvement are defined in detail during Pareto analysis. Sometimes, in that procedure, several kinds of minor stoppages are itemized within the same group of phenomena.

For example, a group may include two minor stoppages described as *parts get caught in chute* and *parts get caught in parts feeder*; but at this point they should be defined more precisely, using descriptions such as

parts get caught at chute connection point 1, or
parts get caught at pattern A segment of parts feeder

If you say only that *parts get caught in the chute*, you fail to specify any particular phenomenon and are only indicating one that occurs somewhere in the chute. In planning improvements, such a vaguely described problem cannot be the target. Instead, there must be specific references to individual phenomena and their corresponding causes. When it is time to analyze the results, you will not get far in the search for causes if you have not done the necessary groundwork in defining individual phenomena.

STEP 5-2: OBSERVE COMPLETED PHENOMENA

This activity involves a detailed observation of the target process or equipment after a minor stoppage has occurred. As such, it is similar to the inspections of the workplace that are typically made right after an accident. It's also much like an examination of the physical appearance of a defective product.

In any minor stoppage situation, there are numerous conditions that could be examined, but the following examples point to a methodology that can be used for selecting the significant ones.

Observation of completed phenomena

Example 1: Parts Get Caught, Jammed, or Wedged in the Feeder Chute

Parts Get Caught

- What feature of the part gets caught on what feature of the chute? If possible, take a photograph of the problem.
- What kind of dents or protrusions exist in that particular segment of the chute? Use a magnifying glass to inspect them.
- Describe the features of those parts which tend to get caught.

Parts Get Jammed

- On what segment of the chute does the first part get caught?
- What kind of configuration do the jammed parts form together?
- Are there any cracks or gaps in which parts can get caught?

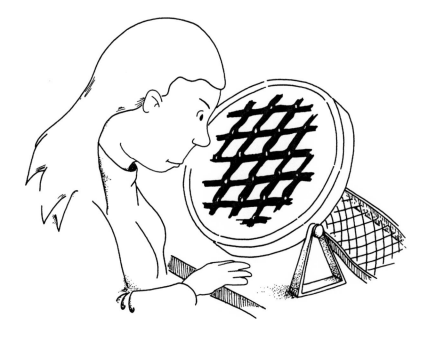

Magnifying glass

- Have any segments of the chute been magnetized?

Parts Get Wedged

- How do the parts become wedged (unable to be gently pressed onward)?
- What is the condition of the side guides on the chute where the parts get wedged?
- Measure and compare the width of the parts with the width of the chute side guides.

Example 2: Parts Leave Their Normal Route as They Are Fed Through the Process

Ejected Parts

- Where do the parts leave the normal route, and to where do they fall?

- Are these *ejected* parts different in any way from the other parts?
- What happens to the parts immediately behind the ejected parts?

Flipped Parts

- Where and in which direction do parts get flipped?
- Are the flipped parts different in any way from the other parts?

Example 3: During Sorting and Aligning of Parts, Some Are Misaligned

- In what way are the parts misaligned?
- Are the misaligned parts different in any way from the other parts?

Example 4: Two or More Parts Leave a Process Together Instead of as Discrete Units

This problem can have different causes depending on the nature of the part. For example, two or more small springs can get tangled together, or two or more washers can get stuck together by oil or because of burrs. Whatever the case, the important question to ask is what is holding the parts together.

Example 5: Parts Cannot Be Picked Up Mechanically or by Suction, or They Drop Soon After Being Picked Up

- What is the orientation and other conditions of parts that cannot be picked up?
- What position are they in after they drop?
- How are parts that cannot be picked up different from other parts?

- Are the chucks or suction cups different?
- What are the suction pressure gauge readings?

Example 6: When Parts Are Repositioned, They Slip from Their New Positions

- Where do the parts come to rest relative to their correct position?
- Have any of the chucks or suction nozzles been magnetized?
- Does foreign matter intrude on the positioning surfaces and, if so, what kind is it?

Example 7: During *Angle Indexing*, Parts Slip from Their Correct Positions

- How much and in what directions do the parts slip?
- Were the parts that slipped set correctly in the jig?

STEP 5-3: OBSERVE PROGRESSIVE PHENOMENA

If a minor stoppage is caused by parts getting hung up somewhere along the process, it's relatively easy to obtain information about the phenomena by simply observing them after a minor stoppage has occurred.

However, the required information may not be available through this type of observation if the parts did not get hung up but instead were ejected, dropped while in transit, or were the cause of some other error due to nonstandard positions or motions. In such cases, the error caused by the parts is not necessarily the direct cause of the minor stoppage, and the method of observation must permit you to witness the actual process rather than just the results of the process.

Observation Methods

Observations can be made with the naked eye, a magnifying glass, or a small video camera (normal home-use type). With a video camera, the process can be played back in front of all the team members several times. This is especially useful for examining minor stoppage phenomena that occur infrequently. In addition, the freeze-frame function of a VCR can help you analyze details of motion such as stroke end points in pneumatic cylinders.

High-speed video recording enables you to see motions that are too rapid to be caught by the human eye or by standard, home-use video cameras. Under the proper conditions, high-speed video cameras can record events that occur within just a few milliseconds.

Here are some examples of the types of information obtainable through an observation of progressive phenomena.

Example 1: Parts Get Caught, Jammed, or Wedged

- Can the parts move by themselves or is each part prodded along by the one behind it?
- In what directions do the parts face as they move along?
- Observe what happens right from the beginning of the process.

Example 2: Parts Leave Their Normal Route, Are Ejected, or Flipped Over as They Are Fed Through the Process

- At what stage in their motion do the parts get ejected or flipped over, and what position are they in when it happens?
- Are there any signs that parts are just about to be ejected or flipped over?

**Example 3: During Sorting and
Aligning of Parts, Some are Misaligned**

- What is the position and pattern of the parts as they enter and pass through the sorting area?
- Can the parts move by themselves or is each part prodded along by the one behind it?
- Check how fast the parts are moving as they are sorted and aligned. Are the misaligned parts moving any faster or slower?

**Example 4: Two or More Parts Leave a Process
Together Instead of as Discrete Units**

- Is the separation mechanism malfunctioning, thereby causing the stopper to be late in stopping the second part?
- Are parts that slip by the stopper moving faster than parts that get stopped?
- Are parts that slip by the stopper attached in some way to the adjacent parts?

**Example 5: Parts Cannot Be Picked Up Mechanically or by
Suction, or They Drop Soon After Being Picked Up**

- Do the chucks or suction cups move the parts at all?
- How far do the parts get raised before they fall?
- Does the part below the top one ever get stuck to it?
- From what part of the chuck or suction cup does the part begin to slip?
- At what point in transit do the parts fall?
- When the parts fall, against what do they fall?
- Onto what section of the parts do the chucks or suction cups hold?

***Example 6: When Parts Are Repositioned,
They Slip from Their New Positions***

- Are the parts positioned correctly before they begin to slip?
- At what point does the slipping begin?

STEP 5-4: ANALYZE OCCURRENCE TRENDS

At this step, search for trends in the occurrence of minor stoppages. The purpose is to provide statistical data to back up the engineering-based search for direct causes. Although these statistics will not reveal individual slight defects, they will help provide a better understanding of the main causal mechanisms.

For example, consider an operation involving a cylinder-driven, automatic unloader that uses a pneumatic-hydraulic convertor. This operation is plagued by a particular problem which occurs sporadically, so an improvement team decides to see if the occurrence of the problem is associated with any time-related variables. They discover that the problem tends to occur before dawn during winter, but does not occur during warmer seasons. This statistic leads to the hypothesis that lubricant in the convertor thickens in cold weather, thereby slowing down the operation of the cylinder actuator and producing the problem.

The occurrence of minor stoppages can be studied and analyzed in relation to several variables, some of which are described in the following text.

Time

Operating conditions vary according to the time of day, the time of year, and even according to the shift. Asking the following questions may prove useful.

Do minor stoppages tend to occur more frequently just before changeover (retooling for different models) and more randomly during normal operation periods? Do they occur more frequently immediately after operations are started than they do during normal operations later in the day? Is there any difference between occurrence trends on different shifts? Is there any difference between the occurrence trends for different seasons?

Equipment

Variations in equipment conditions include differences not only in the main parts of the equipment but also in the molds, jigs, cutting tools, and other related parts.

Check for different minor stoppage occurrence trends among different equipment units (newer and older units, different models, and so on). Even if equipment units are identical, different molds or jigs might still account for variations in occurrence trends. Even if molds or jigs are identical, there may be different conditions (such as dirt or debris) that also affect the trends. Variation in the condition of tools may also affect the frequency of minor stoppages. An example is the sharpness of a cutting tool.

Materials

Different lots of materials, even of the same type, may produce different occurrence trends. Check for variations in occurrence trends for the same type of part provided by different suppliers. If the same type of parts are supplied by the same supplier, check for differences among lots.

Models

Check for occurrence trend differences in similar parts that are used for different models.

Personnel

Check for differences in minor stoppage occurrence trends that can be linked to different equipment operators or setup workers.

STEP 5-5: ANALYZE CURRENT TREATMENT OF PHENOMENA

At this step, analyze how the operators respond when minor stoppages occur. For example, they may slow down the operating speed of the equipment, or they may check and adjust clearances between certain equipment parts.

As with the analysis of occurrence trends, this type of analysis does not teach much about slight defects, but it does help develop an understanding of the basic structure of cause-and-effect relationships.

In the example previously described, a cylinder-driven auto unloader malfunctions when lubricant thickens in the pneumatic-hydraulic convertor. This tends to occur before dawn in the winter months, and it produces an operational error. The current action taken by the operators to rectify this situation is to open the speed controller each time the error occurs. However, if the speed controller is not reset when ambient temperature rises, a different type of operational error will occur.

Information about current responses adds to an understanding of the hypothetical main causal mechanism behind the operational error.

12

Step 6:
Analyze Causes (Step B)

With the knowledge gained at step 4 (*study and inspect target process*) and the factual information obtained at step 5 (*analyze results*) it is now time to look for specific causes. This step is also known as step B (for *breakdown*), and the procedure is one of considering various hypotheses about cause-and-effect relationships.

THE SEARCH FOR CAUSES

In searching for the causes of minor stoppages, it is very important that the actual minor stoppage phenomena be observed. However, no matter how carefully this is done, there may be some conditions that are simply not visible, so not all causes can be confirmed by direct observation. Furthermore, when observing the equipment, you cannot expect to be aided by people describing it to you as they would at a trade fair. Be inquisitive and use your head.

An intellectual search

Engineering Approach and Statistical Approach

Manufacturing processes are the fruit of industrial science and engineering research. The statistical approach to analyzing and solving problems in manufacturing processes is important, but not as centrally important as the engineering approach. However, both are necessary for solving process problems. The statistical approach has the advantage of being a very logical one, but it is seldom incisive enough to produce solutions to problems without the help of the engineering approach. A later section of this book describes how the engineering approach can be used to solve various *phenomena points*.

Breakdown of Causes

Most abnormalities have several causes, some of which have a greater impact than others. Describing these causes in detail is a complicated task, but it is easier if they are divided into two categories: *direct* and *background*. To understand the difference between these, consider the previously described example of the pneumatic cylinder. After research, the team may have discovered that the direct cause of the slow cylinder operation was an inadequate supply of operating oil. Several conditions could exist as background causes for this problem, such as unclear instructions for routine maintenance, an undetected oil leak, or failure of staff to carry out the proper inspections.

The causes of abnormalities are like complex chains, and there are various methods for determining where the direct cause stops and the background cause begins. One method is as follows.

If, for the abnormality to be eliminated, the cause must be improved or corrected within a short period of time, it is considered a *direct* cause. If the abnormality can be eliminated even if the cause is left uncorrected for the time being, the cause is considered *background*. However, if left indefinitely, such background causes lead to the recurrence of direct causes.

Mechanisms

Causes may also be classified as either *main* or *supporting*. Supporting causes are relatively minor ones that serve to reinforce the effect of the main cause or causes. In addition, there may be causes that do not reinforce the main cause but rather contribute in some minor way to the abnormality. These may be termed *secondary* causes, but for the sake of simplicity, they are included here as supporting causes.

For any process, the causal mechanism is the set of causal factors that answers the questions *what* and *how* with regard to the cause-and-effect relationships behind an abnormality in that process.

Many factories use the *fishbone diagram* to chart causal factors. Such diagrams do a good job of answering the *what* question but do almost nothing to answer the *how* question. But to fully understand the delicate phenomena that relate to abnormalities, you must understand the *how*.

Approach to Determining Causes

The key points of the approach to determining the causes of minor stoppages are as follows.

Understand that minor stoppages are caused by slight defects. Suppose that, in a particular process, almost all of the conditions are normal and the process is usually error-free. However, once in a while, a certain number of changes in those conditions, or certain slight defects produce an operation error that results in a minor stoppage.

Understand causes as causal mechanisms. If the cause of an operational error is immediately apparent, then take corrective action immediately. Every equipment operator has experience in taking simple corrective measures for simple errors. But what about minor stoppages for which causes are not so easy to understand? In these cases, rethink your approach to looking for causes. Instead of simply asking *what* caused the stoppage, ask *how* — in other words, by what mechanism — did the causes produce the minor stoppage?

Who is the real criminal?

Determine main causes. Most quality problems and equipment problems stem from several causes, and minor stoppage problems are no exception. However, it is rare that all of the several causes contribute equally to the problem. Some causes are more important than others, so start by working to find the main cause or causes before looking for those less important.

Determine supporting causes. By eliminating the main causes, you will achieve a reduction in minor stoppages. Occasionally, this is even enough to reduce stoppages to the target $1/20$ level, or even down to zero. Usually, however, taking care of the main causes will reduce them by only about one-half at most. Therefore, always deal with the supporting causes as well.

Determine background causes. Make improvements by eliminating the direct causes. However, if you do not bother to find out what background causes helped to create the direct causes, they could create them anew, and you could be faced with the same problems all over again.

STEP 6-1: FIND MAIN CAUSAL MECHANISMS

Using the earlier analogy of the investigation of a crime, the objective now is to go to the scene of the crime (direct causes) and find out who is the main culprit (main cause) and how the crime was committed (how the mechanism works).

Often, the minor stoppage problem can be easily solved once the main causal mechanism is understood. However, finding this mechanism — determining *how* the various causes function to produce the problem — can be a very difficult part of the search. But it is a very important part, and one that can make the difference between success and failure.

Carrying Out the Search

When searching for the main causal mechanism, use both the fact-checking approach and the logical (hypothesizing) approach (see Figure 12-1).

The example of the auto unloader can be used to illustrate the method of searching for the main causal mechanism. This example is so simple that some readers may find the step-by-step description frustratingly slow. However, as mentioned in the preface, it is best to take things slowly and carefully in order to ensure understanding.

Study the Phenomena

As described in Chapter 11, the best place to begin a search for the main causal mechanism is with a careful observation of the phenomena.

Start the Engineering Approach from Phenomena Points

Phenomena points are the local physical factors created by abnormality phenomena. The engineering approach begins with the study of these points.

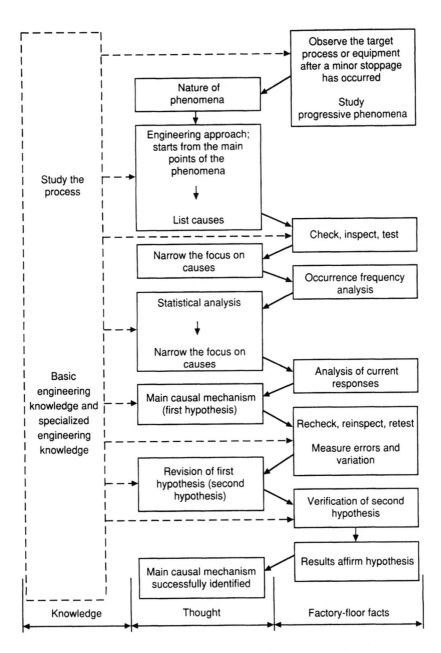

Figure 12-1. Implementation of Search for Main Causal Mechanism

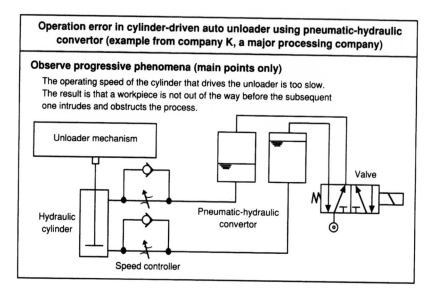

Operation error in cylinder-driven auto unloader using pneumatic-hydraulic convertor (example from company K, a major processing company)

Observe progressive phenomena (main points only)

The operating speed of the cylinder that drives the unloader is too slow. The result is that a workpiece is not out of the way before the subsequent one intrudes and obstructs the process.

Figure 12-2. Drive System for Unloader

In this example, the operating speed of the hydraulic cylinder is reduced, and this leads to abnormalities (see Figure 12-2). The cylinder consists of an oil input system, a convertor made up of a cylinder and piston, and an output system made up of a piston rod.

Engineering approach for phenomena points

Reason for reduced speed of cylinder operation (one part only)

Oil input system
- Reduction in pneumatic pressure, the drive power source
- Increase in oil flow resistance in pneumatic-hydraulic convertor and subsequent parts
  - Clogged pipes and valves
  - Thickening of oil

Convertor system (cylinder and piston)
- Internal leak due to packing wear

Output system (piston rod)
- Greater operational resistance in mechanism linked to piston rod

The first step is to reexamine the phenomena that have already been understood through observation. This is basically a repeat of step 4 (study and inspect the target process), and it requires not only a basic understanding of the target process, but also some general knowledge of industrial engineering.

The next step is to list systematically all causes noted during the study of the general nature of the phenomena. This is usually quite easy to do, as the following example shows.

Check, Study, and Test Engineering Approach Results

At this step, use the target equipment to test the results of the engineering-based determination of phenomena points. Begin with a cleaning inspection, a relatively simple way of checking results. If possible, carry out equipment tests to verify the causes. Even after testing and studying the phenomena points, some uncertainties may remain. At this point, do not try to resolve these uncertainties, but continue with the investigation.

Checking, studying, and testing engineering approach results for phenomena points

- Reduction in pneumatic pressure (main power source). If there is a pressure gauge, use it to check air pressure immediately. If there is no pressure gauge, this remains unresolved.

- Increased oil flow resistance in pneumatic-hydraulic convertor and subsequent parts; not visible from outside.
  - Clogged pipes and valves. Must disassemble to inspect.
  - Thickening of oil. Must measure oil thickness.

- Internal leak due to packing wear. Not visible from outside.

- Greater operational resistance in mechanism linked to piston rod. Disconnect power source and operate manually to do a general check and to determine if it is a main cause. If it cannot be checked manually, the question remains unresolved.

"Simple test"
Set speed controller for higher speed and check cylinder operation rate. This test checks for increase in oil flow resistance in pneumatic-hydraulic convertor and subsequent parts.

Statistical Approach Based on Occurrence Trend Analysis

The statistical approach helps confirm or eliminate the possible causes suggested by results of occurrence trend analysis as described in Chapter 11. This enables you to narrow the focus and concentrate on the relevant causes, and it also clarifies some things about uncertain items. For instance, it will help you decide whether further checks need to be made by means such as disassembly inspections.

> Occurrence trend analysis ⟶ Statistical approach
> Tends to occur before dawn during coldest months. Does not occur during warm seasons.
>
> ---
>
> Occurrence trend suggests that there is an increase in oil flow resistance in the pneumatic-hydraulic convertor and subsequent parts. This is thought to be due to thickening of the oil.
>
> Finding this solution depends on knowing that the thickness of oil increases as temperature drops.

What is needed at this point is a hands-on or engineering-based confirmation of the facts. For example, measure the drop in temperature before dawn in the coldest months and then determine the exact correlation between ambient temperature and oil thickness. Do this with a line graph or other statistical tools.

Use Results of Current Response Analysis

Information gained from the analysis of current responses (see Chapter 11) can help determine the main causes. It can also help develop a hypothesis of the main causal mechanism as shown in the example on the opposite page.

Disassembly Inspection, Error and Variation Measurement

Now perform some detailed checking of the target equipment based on your hypothesis of the main causal mechanism.

Current response

• If operational errors start to occur, use speed controller to accelerate cylinder operation. When operational errors stop, do not forget to reset the speed controller for slower operation, or else other errors will occur when ambient temperature rises.

Checking (question and answer)

Q: Why will other operational errors occur when ambient temperature rises if the speed controller is not reset?

A: Operational errors will occur because of cylinder overspeed.

Causal mechanism (hypothesis)

• Based on current information, the following primary hypothesis can be proposed for the causal mechanism: When ambient temperature drops, the oil thickens, which slows down cylinder movement and results in operational errors.

Begin by performing a second cleaning inspection in case something was omitted from the first one. Then retest the equipment. If this is still not enough to clarify and confirm the cause of the operational error, take further steps.

For example, it may be necessary to disassemble and inspect the valve to check for clogging or deterioration, measure the precision of the equipment, or check the dimensional precision of parts for any variations from the standard.

Review and Verification of Hypothesis

If the information obtained so far does not agree perfectly with your hypothesis of the main causal mechanism, review the hypothesis and come up with another one. To verify the hypothesis, conduct tests aimed at duplicating the operational error phenomena based on your hypothesis. If they are successful, consider your hypothesis to be correct. If the tests fail to duplicate the phenomena, repeat the entire procedure and come up with a different hypothesis. If there appears to be no way to verify the hypothesis in this manner, continue on to the next step without such verification.

Examples of Main Causal Mechanisms

The following are two examples of main causal mechanisms.

Example 1: Transistor Caught at Chute Connection

Figure 12-3 is a diagram of the target process. At a point close to the parts-fastening head, two individual segments of the chute abut and are secured to each other. It is at this point that some of the transistors get caught up.

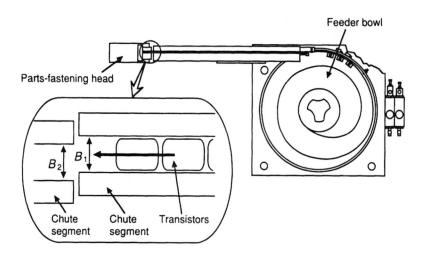

Figure 12-3. Slight Gap at Chute Connection

The two direct causal factors behind the resulting minor stoppage are the slight gap in the chute connection and the small burrs on some of the transistors. Together, these two direct causal factors constitute the main cause. You now know *what* the mechanism is. *How* the mechanism works can be explained as a type of entanglement in which a slightly burred transistor gets caught in the gap in the chute connection, as illustrated in Figure 12-4 and described in Figure 12-5.

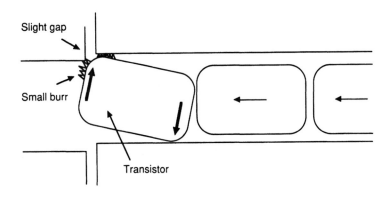

Figure 12-4. Entanglement Phenomenon

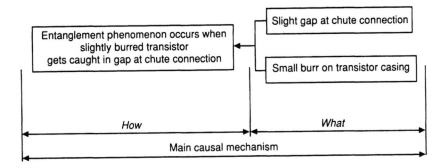

Figure 12-5.   Main Causal Mechanism: Transistor Caught at Chute Connection

Example 2: Spring Assembly Error

Automatic assembly of springs usually involves many difficulties, especially if the springs are small. Consider a minor stoppage error that occurs at an automatic assembly process for small springs with coil width of 4.0 millimeters and wire width of 0.5 millimeters. The process has four main operations.

1. A spring is fed to the process through a pneumatic tube.
2. A hook catcher snags one of the hooks on the spring, then the hook turns (of its own weight) to a horizontal

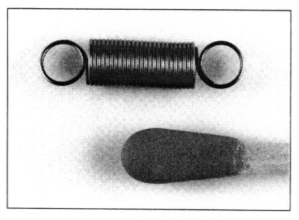

Figure 12-6. Spring

position (hereafter this shall be called *horizontal turning*).
3. A spring assembly pin is lowered to grab hold of the spring hook.
4. The spring assembly pin pulls the spring to the component onto which it is supposed to be hooked.

To some extent, the operational errors are caused when the spring hook does not turn completely horizontal. Figures 12-6, 12-7, and 12-8 illustrate and describe this problem.

Methods for Investigating Main Causal Mechanism

Investigate the main causal mechanism by studying the nature of the minor stoppage using any of the following three methods.

- Method A: Observation of completed phenomena
- Method B: Observation of progressive phenomena
- Method C: Hypothesis

Method A: Observation of Completed Phenomena

In cases such as the chute connection example described earlier, use the *observation of completed phenomena* method. To do

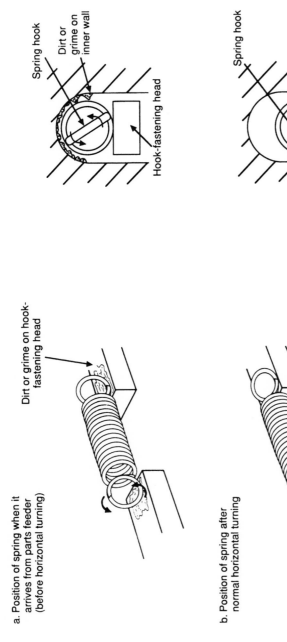

Spring hook

Dirt or grime on inner wall

Hook-fastening head

Spring hook

Dirt or grime on hook-fastening head

a. Position of spring when it arrives from parts feeder (before horizontal turning)

b. Position of spring after normal horizontal turning

Figure 12-7. Horizontal Turning of Spring Hook

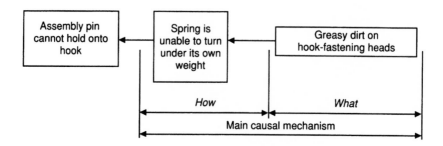

Figure 12-8. Main Causal Mechanism of Spring Assembly Error

so, examine the slight gap in the chute connection and the small burr on the first entangled transistor — in other words, the causal mechanism described in Figure 12-5. At this point, it might be assumed the mystery of the minor stoppages has been solved.

However, even before this investigation began, someone may have noticed the gap in the chute connection but not have suspected that it was the cause of minor stoppage problems. Operators watch and handle the same equipment day in and day out, but they are not likely to pay close attention to such things as chute connections, or wonder about any slight gaps they may notice. But operators *must* be encouraged to develop a sharp eye for these slight defects. When the parts are very small, operators must learn to be extremely sensitive, watching and listening for the slightest changes in conditions.

The entanglement phenomenon shown in Figure 12-4 is not something that is likely to be noticed just through observation or even by disassembly inspection. The most likely initial hypothesis about the causal mechanism behind this problem would be that the small burrs on the transistors make them more resistant to sliding down the vibrating chute. The obvious response would, of course, be to increase the vibration force. When this response does not solve the entanglement problem but only produces new problems related to stronger vibration, it becomes necessary to reconsider the first hypothesis and form a more advanced, secondary one.

Method B: Observation of Progressive Phenomena

This method was used in the example for which the main causal mechanism was found to be the reduced speed of a cylinder (see Figure 12-2). As mentioned earlier, when an error is caused by nonstandard positions or motions, and it is necessary to observe the actual process rather than just the result of the process, the *observation of progressive phenomena* method is the most effective one to use for determining the main causal mechanism.

Method C: Hypothesis

When neither method A nor method B is feasible, or when they are feasible but do not provide enough information, resort to method C — hypothesizing.

In the example of the spring assembly error, the main causal mechanism was determined by hypothesis (see Figure 12-8). In this case, since the hook-fastening head is made of metal, there is no way to see through it. If method A is followed and the hook-fastening head is disassembled for inspection, the abnormal conditions that must be observed are destroyed. Thus, you are forced to resort to hypothesizing.

STEP 6-2: VERIFY MAIN CAUSAL MECHANISMS

Without an accurate understanding of the main causal mechanism, there is little chance of success in solving the problem behind the minor stoppage. When your understanding of the main causal mechanism is based on observation of progressive phenomena or on a hypothesis, be sure to verify it. There is no need to verify all the little details; just find evidence that your understanding of the mechanism in general is correct.

Check the evidence against the facts

Check the Analysis of Results

Check the hypothetical main causal mechanism against the facts obtained through observation of completed phenomena, observation of progressive phenomena, or data obtained from occurrence trend analysis. If these checks reveal serious contradictions or inconsistencies, review the hypothesis and find a better one.

Verify Through Testing

The best way to verify is through testing.

One method is to intentionally re-create the causes to see whether they produce the same phenomena. For example, if you have hypothesized that burred parts are getting caught in a chute, find or manufacture burred parts and send them down the chute to see what happens. Likewise, if the hypothesis involves magnetized springs, magnetize some springs and see whether they cause the expected problems.

In addition, always verify experimentally by taking the opposite approach: set up conditions that exclude all those hypothesized as contributing to the main causal mechanism, and then check to make sure the problem does *not* occur. Once again, consider the example in which burred parts get caught in the chute. Do a thorough, full-lot inspection to make sure none of the parts are burred, then send them down the chute. Note that much fewer get caught than before. This indicates that although you are correct in hypothesizing that burrs are the main causal mechanism, they are not the only cause; there are others that should be identified and eliminated as well.

If verification is impossible because the duplication tests prove inconclusive or they are impossible to set up, stick with your hypothesis and proceed to the next step, which is to try improvement measures. In this case, regard these measures as a sort of verification testing.

STEP 6-3: MEASURE DIFFERENCES AND VARIATIONS

Qualitative methods of investigation such as cleaning inspection, disassembly inspection, and simple tests may not lead to any conclusions about causes. Or they may vaguely suggest causes but not provide enough information with which to begin improvement activities. In these cases, measure or otherwise search for errors and variations that may bring the causes into sharper focus.

Measurement of Equipment Precision

Errors and variation in equipment indicate a lack of dynamic or static precision conditions. The following sections show how such precision problems can lead to conveyance errors.

Precision of Mechanical Position

Imprecise positioning of workpieces by mechanical devices can have several causes, as follows.

Inaccurate values. The example of the slight gap in the chute connection is a case of inaccurate values. Specifically, the

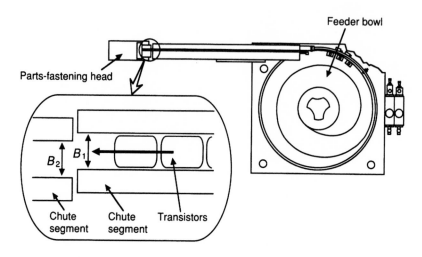

Figure 12-9. Slight Gap at Chute Connection

gap was caused by a slight error in the positioning of the through hole for the screw mechanism (see Figure 12-9).

Position layout precision. If the process uses a robot that picks up parts from rows of parts delivered on pallets, check the precision of the coordinate points where the robot fingers move. There may be problems that are being caused by slight imprecision in the finger movements. Sometimes, such motions start out quite accurately but gradually lose precision.

Precision of repeated motions. When *pick and place* robots or other equipment that picks things up and puts them down is being used, there may be variation in the precision of repeated motions. For instance, a robot might follow the same motion command 10 times but not with equal precision each time. This kind of precision can and should be measured.

Looseness in mechanisms. Loose mechanisms can be a cause of variation in the precision of motions. Looseness in a mechanism is best measured quantitatively as an index of static strength. Figure 12-10 illustrates this.

In this example, take the following two measurements.

First, add a specified weight (for example, 500 grams) to the

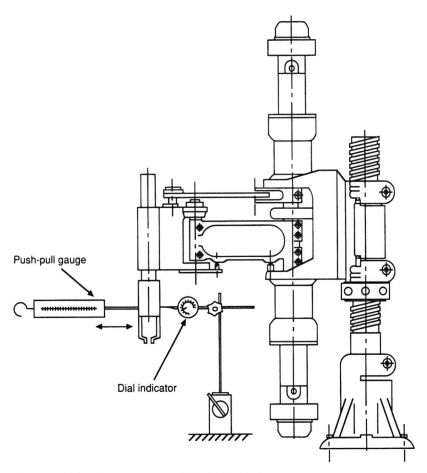

Figure 12-10. Measurement of Static Strength

vertical portion of the arm. Note and record gauge reading for arm position. Add a second weight, leave it in place for a few moments, then remove it. Measure the new arm position, and compare it with the initial position to see if any variation exists. Such variation indicates *looseness* due to lack of static strength.

Mechanical Timing Precision

When mechanical movements are performed at high speeds, minor stoppages often arise from operational timing errors, gaps, or variation between mechanisms.

These timing-related problems are relatively rare among slower-moving mechanisms such as gears, cams, and mechanical links; however, they are becoming increasingly common among today's more advanced automated equipment models. This is not only because the operations are considerably faster (on the order of milliseconds) but also because the equipment models include more pneumatic cylinders and suction devices that are easily plagued by variations in response time.

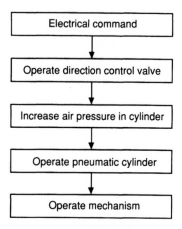

Figure 12-11. Operation Steps for Pneumatic Device

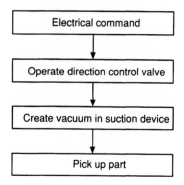

Figure 12-12. Operation Steps for Suction Device

For example, consider Figure 12-11, which shows the series of operations for a pneumatic cylinder, and Figure 12-12, which shows the operational steps for a suction device.

Electrical Timing Precision

Microswitches and other electrical devices operate at very high speeds, so even when response instability causes errors, this seldom affects the the response time or other timing factors. However, with the ongoing trend toward computer-controlled equipment, a lot of unexpected kinds of errors are occurring because of faulty signal timing caused by software bugs (that is, slight defects).

In some types of high-speed automated assembly equipment, there have been problems with unstable timing. In one such case, the equipment operator used a synchroscope to chart the problem, as shown in Figure 12-13.

Measurement of Parts Variation

Consider the previous example of burrs on transistor casings. First establish several levels of burr sizes, then measure the

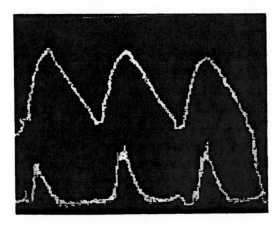

Figure 12-13. Synchroscope Analysis

burrs and analyze the distribution of sizes. With this information, calculate the likelihood of different burr sizes getting caught in the chute. During the improvement-making steps, this information can be used as support data.

By measuring the dimensional distribution of the various parts (such as transistors, chip capacitors, and chip resistors) that will be sent down the chute, you can judge the likelihood of each type of part getting caught.

STEP 6-4: LOOK FOR SUPPORTING MECHANISMS

Not only main causes but also supporting causes must be addressed to achieve high improvement goals. If your intention is to cut minor stoppages by only about one-half, then address only the main causes. However, if you intend to reduce them to $\frac{1}{20}$ their original level, address both main and supporting causes.

Definition of Supporting Causes

Supporting causes are those that reinforce the effect of the main cause or causes. Basically, they are of three types: *joint, supporting,* and *secondary.*

Joint causes support the main cause to either make minor stoppages possible or to increase their frequency.

Some supporting causes enter through *unlocked doors.* For example, some abnormalities occur as a result of conditions brought about by inadequate preventive measures. In such cases, the supporting cause is the problem that enters through the *unlocked door* of inadequate preventive measures or oversights that made those measures less than adequate.

Finally, there are supporting causes that do not support the main cause directly but instead contribute in some minor way to the abnormality. These can be referred to as secondary causes.

Joint causes

Example of Supporting Causal Mechanism

The method for studying both the main and supporting causal mechanisms is basically the same.

In the earlier example of spring assembly errors (see Figure 12-8), the improvement team had proposed and checked the hypothesis that the main causal mechanism behind the spring assembly error was grimy dirt on the hook-fastening head. However, this hypothesis alone did not solve the problem. Later, they found out that a small dent existed in the hook-fastening head, and this may have been preventing the spring hook from turning to a fully horizontal position. This second hypothesis turned out to be correct.

The small dent in the hook-fastening head should be regarded as a supporting causal mechanism. In other words, the main hypothesis was still the fact that there was dirt on the head; the problem of the small dent only added to the main problem of the dirt. This supporting causal mechanism is illustrated in Figures 12-14 and 12-15.

Supporting causes that enter through unlocked doors

The team noted that even dealing with the small dent and the dirt on the hook-fastening head was not enough to completely solve the problem. After studying the situation further, they discovered that the hook-fastening stands had been magnetized. The spring weighs about 200 milligrams, and at this light weight, even a little magnetization at the hook contact

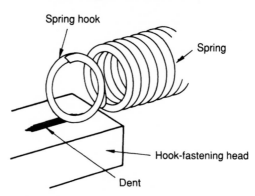

Figure 12-14. Spring Assembly

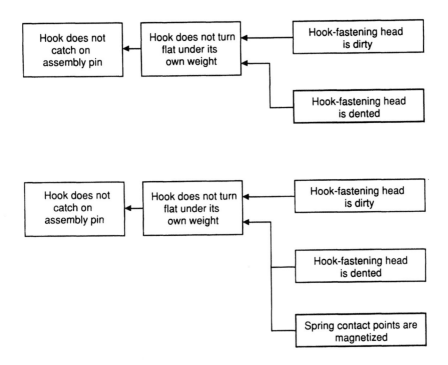

Figure 12-15. Spring Assembly Error

points is enough to interfere with the natural tendency of the spring to turn to a horizontal position in which the hooks are flat on the hook-fastening heads. Thus, the group found a second supporting cause — magnetization (see Figure 12-16).

As it turned out, there were three supporting causes in this example.

The team made an improvement that got rid of the second supporting cause. This helped reduce the number of errors but did not succeed in completely eliminating them. The team knew that they either had to find some other minor cause for the failure of the spring to turn horizontal, or they had to continue manually aiding the spring rotation. They studied the situation some more, and finally noticed that the problem was in the shape of the hook-fastening head. They realized that the shape most conducive to spring rotation was not a flat head but rather

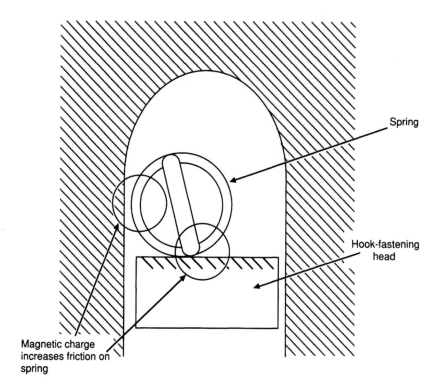

Figure 12-16. Spring Assembly: Magnetization of Hook-fastening Stand

a convex one. After making this improvement, they found that the problem was almost completely eliminated. Figure 12-17 describes the mechanism of this third supporting cause and Figure 12-18 illustrates the corresponding improvement. This cause should be regarded as a slight defect in the design of the equipment.

Even though the flatness of the hook-fastening head contributed very little to the friction resistance against the spring rotation, the other causes — namely, the dirt, dent, and magnetization — *opened the door* for this minor factor to function as a supporting causal mechanism behind the spring-fastening error.

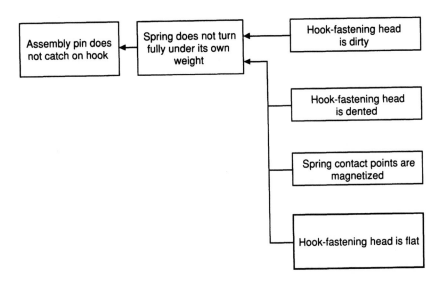

Figure 12-17. Spring Assembly Error: Supporting Causal Mechanism

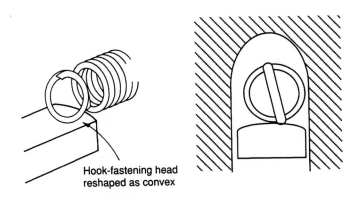

Figure 12-18. Spring Assembly Improvement: Convex Shape of Hook-fastening Head

Approach to Supporting Causes

Naturally, you always hope for an approach that leads, like a railroad track, straight to the causes you are seeking. However, finding causes usually requires a lot of care and tenacity. Closely observe the current conditions and error-related phenomena, get your hands dirty in cleaning and inspecting the equipment, and think about the facts.

Points for Finding Supporting Causes

The following points are helpful in the search for supporting causes, and should be committed to memory.

- Assume that supporting causes exist.
- Recognize that abnormalities cannot be thoroughly eliminated unless supporting causes are found and removed.
- Recognize the types of supporting causes: joint causes, supporting causes that enter through unlocked doors, and secondary causes.

Pattern for Finding Supporting Causes

There is a pattern for finding causal mechanisms that include not only the main cause or causes but also the supporting causes. If you can use this pattern, do so, since it is the quickest way to make improvements, and in most cases it is the best possible approach.

However, this pattern has a weak point: it does not permit verification of the specific effects of each type of cause. Be conscious of this fact if such verification becomes necessary.

The pattern is basically an improvement cycle that consists of the following steps: (1) look for the slight defects that make up the main cause or causes, (2) make the corresponding improvement, and (3) check the results. If the results are successful, start the improvement cycle over again, this time to find and remove slight defects that function as supporting causes.

Although this pattern takes more time than the general pattern does, it has the advantage of being a more effective and verifiable way of making improvements.

Always go after the main causes first, then the supporting causes. This is because the effects of the supporting causes cannot be seen as clearly when the main causes still exist, so it becomes difficult to check the results of supporting cause improvements.

No one is perfect, so you can never be sure that every slight defect has been uncovered. Make defects as easy as possible to identify by first dealing with the main causes, so that the supporting causes will then be easier to find. In the example of the spring assembly error, if the team had begun by thinking that magnetization was the main problem, their improvement effort would have had little, if any, effect. In fact, the effects of the magnetization were largely hidden by the problem of dirt on the hook-fastening head. Once the dirt problem was solved, they were able to obtain a quantitative understanding of the magnetization problem.

STEP 6-5: LOOK FOR BACKGROUND CAUSES

Find and eliminate background causes, which are background conditions that contribute to the creation of direct and supporting causes. This process is like finding out why a criminal committed a crime or why the door was left unlocked.

Figure 12-19 shows how an improvement team studied the background causes that explain the existence of the main cause, which is a slight gap in the chute connection.

Dealing with a background cause prevents the direct causes from developing again. If you merely wanted to eliminate the slight gap in the chute connection (see Figure 12-9), you could modify the widths of the upper and lower chute segments (B1 and B2) and train the retooling workers to pay closer attention when positioning them. Such measures may be successful for a short time, but in a mass-production situation their effects will not last long, for the following reason: Even though chute segments are now fabricated to have matching widths, no one knows why they fell out of tolerance in the first place. The possibility of fabricating more defective chutes still exists. Furthermore, advising retooling workers to be more careful about positioning the chutes will not prevent variation in retooling precision based on idiosyncratic differences among workers. In other words, the improvement in retooling will probably not last long either. In summary, these improvements do not thoroughly eliminate the causes of the minor stoppages.

Therefore, be very much aware that finding and removing background causes is a necessary part of making thorough improvements that effectively prevent the recurrence of the original problem.

Background causes

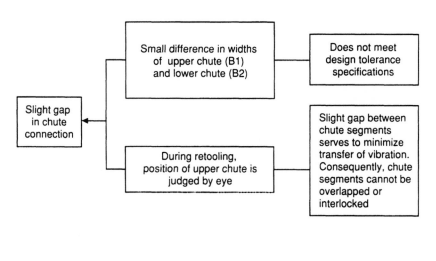

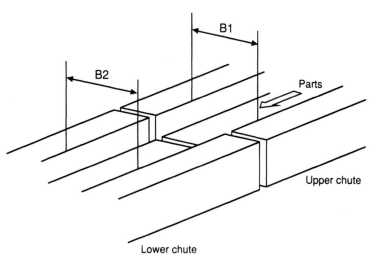

Figure 12-19. Development of Background Cause

13

Step 7:

Apply PDC Cycle to Make Improvements (Step C)

This step consists of establishing an improvement policy and applying the PDC (plan-do-check) cycle to make specific improvements. This step is also known as step C (for *create*) since it is here that the creative process of drafting improvement plans begins.

STEP 7-1: ESTABLISH IMPROVEMENT POLICY

Accurately identifying all causes and eliminating them solves the minor stoppage problem. However, this is usually much easier said than done because difficult conditions often stand in the way. The actual work of making improvements entails overcoming these conditions by developing improvement plans that are both technically and economically feasible. The purpose of the improvement policy is to establish a framework for success based on realism. It is, basically, an orientation to planning the improvement strategy.

Take the following steps when establishing an improvement policy.

Policy

- Discriminate between prior conditions and causes.
- Deal only with causes related to the target process.
- Start with the biggest causes first (the ones with the strongest effects).
- Select causes by affirmation and negation.
- Work for thorough improvements.

Each of these points is discussed in the following sections.

Discriminate Between Prior Conditions and Causes

Consider the previously described example in which the operation of a cylinder is slower than normal during cold winter months. The main causal mechanism for this operational error was hypothesized as a decrease in temperature resulting in thickening of operating oil.

The primary cause was seen as the drop in ambient temperature that occurs just before dawn during the cold winter months. Other linked causes included faulty operation of the auto unloader. For this purpose, it is perfectly fine to regard a drop in temperature as a cause; however, what can the improvement team do about the weather? This is a natural phenomenon, so when planning improvements, consider it not as a *cause* but as a *prior condition*.

The cause of the slow cylinder problem is not the cold air. It is the failure to design equipment than can tolerate such cold conditions. According to Professor Nakaigawa, abnormal phenomena are conditions resulting from causes rooted in human behavior. We must accept that responsibility. Human behavior is the ultimate cause of operational errors.

Deal Only with Causes Related to the Target Process

Some causes belong to the target process, while others do not. Causes that do not belong are those resulting from problems with another process. These may be variations in the quality of the product or in the materials used, but the important point is that these causes do not belong to the target process even though they affect it. They arose out of problems with another process and are, therefore, not *target* causes.

Restricting the target causes to those that relate only to the target process is one of the most important points in establishing an improvement policy. You will fail to make effective improvements if you focus attention on causes related to other processes.

For example, if you stop the production of burred transistors at an upstream process but fail to eliminate the slight gap in the chute connection at the target process, the improvement will not be very effective. Improvements are made by people. If a team establishes an improvement plan such as this, people are not likely to go along with it. They will regard it as a plan drafted by a team that is ignoring the improvement needs of their own process while asking others to work on theirs.

Usually, it is hard to tell before making an improvement how much each of these two types of causes actually contributes to the abnormality phenomena. But by isolating and then dealing with the causes related to the target process, you learn how much the other causes really contribute. This makes clear just how large a scope of causes you are excluding when you deal only with target-related causes. Using the same example of the transistors that get caught up in the chute, once you have an idea of the role played by the gap in the chute connection, you can get a clear picture of the burr size tolerance, which relates to burrs produced at another process.

Start with the Biggest Causes First

Start with the main causes or what you hypothesize them to be. When addressing the joint causes, begin with those estimated to have the greatest effects. Discussed earlier in this book was the need to work from large causes to smaller ones. The main reason is that if you were to work on small causes first, the improvement would have an impact on the problem but probably not one that could be easily measured or quantified. As a result, the improvement efforts would not show discernible results. If people cannot see results, they may lose enthusiasm for making further improvements.

If the main cause is found to be in the target process, there is every reason to adopt an improvement policy of dealing only with the causes related to the target process. If the main cause turns out to be in another process, and it is a rarely occurring quality defect, you should still begin with causes related to the target process.

Select Causes by Affirmation and Negation

The goal should be the elimination of all causes that relate to the target process; however, there are practical restrictions that sometimes make this impossible. This is especially true when it comes to automated equipment and automated lines.

As a general rule, you cannot make successful improvements unless you negate the status quo and avoid complacency. Understand, however, that improvements are not made just by sheer effort.

To begin, assign each cause to one of the following two categories.

1. Causes that can and should be thoroughly eliminated.
2. Causes that for practical reasons cannot be thoroughly eliminated but that can be partly allowed and partly neutralized.

This evaluation must be part of improvement policy-making activities because making an improvement essentially means negating the status quo. Not making an improvement means affirming the causes of abnormalities, and this means affirming the status quo. The following approach is helpful when negation and affirmation are used in improvement policy making.

Obvious quality defects must be eliminated (negated) without exception. Here, there is no room for compromise — the policy must be to eliminate them completely because they undermine established quality standards. It is important to eliminate not only defects that belong to the target process but also those that belong to any upstream process.

This point may seem to contradict a point made earlier about dealing exclusively with causes related to the target process. But there is no such contradiction. Earlier, the emphasis was on the order in which improvements are made — in other words, how to begin by dealing only with the target process. That does not mean that the other processes should never be dealt with; it only means that this should be left for later stages of the improvement program.

There are two ways of dealing with the causes of minor stoppages that are the results of quality defects at processes upstream of the target process. One is to make an improvement at the relevant upstream process, and the other is to modify the target process so that it neutralizes the defect. The first way is obviously the same kind of improvement described in this book, so there is no need to discuss it separately. As for the second way, the required modifications are often too expensive to be practical. They usually involve devices that make the process more complicated rather than simpler, and this adds to the risk of future minor stoppages. Furthermore, this second way does nothing to get at the root of the problem, which is a quality defect at an upstream process.

Some things should be dealt with by partial affirmation and partial neutralization of effects. For example, consider an upstream process at which parts are fabricated. All are within current quality standards, but there is a slight variation in them that must be addressed as a cause of an abnormality in the target process downstream. The option is to apply stricter standards at the upstream process. However, if this is too difficult to implement, consider a policy of neutralizing the effect of the variation by adjusting the target process itself.

Before deciding which way to approach the problem, determine whether the slight variation just described falls into the category of cause or prior condition. If it is a prior condition, realize that, because it falls within quality standards, neutralizing it will have little effect on the causes of the abnormality phenomena in the target process. Use your wits to find a way of eliminating it, and realize that quality standards are not engraved in stone and that there is always room for improvement.

However, a policy of modifying the target process to neutralize the effect of an upstream problem is still probably the best policy in the following situations:

- If the quality defects are in common parts such as semiconductors that meet widely accepted quality standards like those of the JIS (Japanese Industrial Standards).
- If better parts (parts that meet stricter quality standards) are available but are economically unfeasible.
- If improving the quality of the parts requires a significant increase in the degree of precision control at the process where they are used.

Example: Parts supplied to a process where precision control is on the order of 0.1 millimeter require precision control of 0.01 millimeter to achieve the desired quality.

- If significant precision improvements are required on conveyance tools that are being stored in large quantities.

Example: At a process using a robot for autoloading, minor stoppages are being caused by inadequate precision in the pallets that carry the parts. It would cost too much to increase the precision of the pallets, which are cheaply made of styrofoam, and the pallet manufacturer refuses to supply custom-made ones with higher precision just for the sake of a minor stoppage problem. In such cases, it is usually more economical to take other approaches, such as improving the precision control of the robot or devising failsafe measures for the robot fingers.

Work for Thorough Improvements

This means being determined to set and achieve 20-fold increases in MTBF rates by making thorough improvements aimed at each of the minor stoppage phenomena. This is possible only by bringing tenacious determination to the improvement program. Think of thorough improvements as those that completely eliminate minor stoppages. The following text describes some points to keep in mind when planning an improvement program.

The ideal is to restore conditions to the point where minor stoppages no longer occur. Consider an operation in which they do occur frequently as a result of small screws getting caught up in a screw-feeding device. As described in Figure 13-1 and pictured in Figure 13-2, this screw-feeding device consists of several interconnected segments. Here, the best policy is to eliminate all gaps at the connection points to prevent the screws from getting caught (this example is described in detail in case study 18, following).

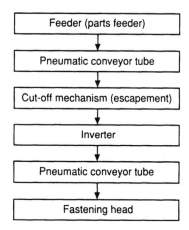

Figure 13-1. Structure of Small Screw Feed Device (Set Screws with Hexagonal Holes)

Another example, described and illustrated in case study 11, following, is an improvement to a chute used for delivering and carrying parts picked up from a pallet. As a result of the improvement, parts no longer became entangled in the chute.

Keep in mind that simply making adjustments is not an improvement measure. Problems such as slight gaps in chute connections can be temporarily solved by making adjustments; however, these cannot be called improvements, because the gaps can still develop and lead to further minor stoppages. Instead, consider improvement measures such as using tele-scopic (insert-type) connections or a gap-checking gauge. Such measures would enable the chutes to remain problem-free after each retooling operation. To borrow a term from automatic con-trol technology, adjustments are a *closed loop* type of control. In other words, try out the equipment, check the results, and if something is wrong, make an adjustment. This process does lit-tle to prevent the occurrence and recurrence of minor stoppages.

If you do an occurrence trend analysis and find that most stoppages occur in the wake of retooling operations, take this as a sign that people are performing adjustments when they should be making improvements.

Figure 13-2. Front End of Automated Screw-fastening Device

Also remember, where applicable, to try to obtain the combined effect of eliminating some causes and neutralizing others. If a cause cannot be totally eliminated, plan to reduce its occurrence as much as possible, and neutralize the occurrences that cannot be eliminated. The combined effect of these two tactics will be an almost complete elimination of the target minor stoppage. Here are two examples of this, both of which were fully described in Chapter 12.

In the case of the transistors getting caught at a chute connection, the improvement is a combined effect of two actions: eliminating all burrs that do not meet current quality standards, and eliminating all gaps in chute connections.

In the case of the spring assembly errors that resulted from the inability of the spring hook to rotate to a horizontal position, the improvement team was able to eliminate friction resistance during rotation of the hook by eliminating dirt, dents, and magnetization on or near the hook-fastening heads. They also changed the profile of the hook-fastening heads to eliminate some of the remaining friction resistance. This improved rotation ability and solved the problem of spring-fastening errors. The modification to the profile of the hook-fastening heads is categorized as a cause neutralization measure.

Example of Improvement Policy Deliberations

The following text describes the steps taken by an improvement team in its effort to understand the mechanisms behind an operational error and formulate an improvement policy to deal with it.

The operational error occurs in a cylinder-driven auto unloader that uses a pneumatic-hydraulic convertor (example from company K, a major processing firm). For further description, see Figure 12-2. The team's hypothesis for the main causal mechanism is as follows:

The operating oil in the pneumatic-hydraulic convertor thickens in cold weather. This slows down the operation of the cylinder actuator, which results in operational errors in the auto unloader. The team noted that opening the oil supply valve eliminated the operational errors; however, other errors occurred if the valve was not tightened during warmer weather. These errors were the result of overspeed operation of the cylinder actuator.

As part of their search for an improvement policy, the team examined several aspects of the operation on the basis of their understanding of it, then considered possible improvements, as follows.

1. The variation in ambient temperature must be regarded as a prior condition. The target operation cannot be air-conditioned to stabilize the functioning of the auto loader.
2. The use of a pneumatic-hydraulic convertor makes the equipment susceptible to the effects of ambient temperature changes. Can the equipment be modified to use a completely pneumatic drive system? Or a completely

electric one? After studying the operation, the team realized that the pneumatic cylinder operates at close to minimum speed, so the pneumatic-hydraulic convertor is necessary to stabilize the operating speed. Switching to an electrical or solenoid-driven system would require extensive remodeling of the equipment.

3. Operational errors occur easily because there is no feedback system to monitor and control the forward and reverse motions of the cylinder. Could such a feedback system be installed as an improvement? Unfortunately, the workpieces are delivered at intervals that have no relation to the operation of the unloader, so a change in the operational timing of the unloader is not an effective improvement.

4. Perhaps the wrong kind of operating oil is being used. Or perhaps the oil is not changed often enough, so it becomes too old and dirty. Further discussion revealed that the problem was not how much the oil thickens in cold weather, but the fact that it thickens at all. Nevertheless, the team decided that a meeting should be arranged with the oil manufacturer to discuss the possible influence of dirty oil and other relevant topics to see if a more suitable type of oil could be found for the target equipment.

5. The speed controller used to regulate the operating oil system is not designed to be a temperature-compensation device. Would it be advisable to install a flow-rate control valve that included a temperature compensation function? This was regarded as probably the best improvement plan. However, there was some doubt about how well the pneumatic-hydraulic convertor would operate with this new device installed. The group decided to consult with the hydraulic equipment manufacturer and conduct some tests.

6. The operating oil system is not protected by a cover, and

is therefore susceptible to ambient temperature changes. Perhaps insulating the operating oil system would solve the problem. The team decided to have the technical staff study the problem of how to insulate against such a large variation in ambient temperature. They had to estimate the costs, including those for heating and insulation. However, in view of the extra cleaning and maintenance involved, the team thought it better to solve the problem using the ideas presented in paragraphs 4 and 5, preceding.

On the basis of their investigation, the team established a workable improvement policy.

Recognizing the change in ambient temperature as a prior condition, they accepted the current conditions for the pneumatic-hydraulic convertor and the control system. With respect to the use of operating oil during the cold months, they suggested that the following improvements be made in the order listed.

1. Look into the possibility of selecting a more suitable operating oil.
2. Study the possibility of using a flow-rate control valve equipped with a temperature compensation function to replace the speed controller.
3. Try to obtain the combined effect of the previous two improvements. If this combined effect does not solve the problem, look into insulation options.

STEP 7-2: APPLY PDC CYCLE

Using the items and sequence established as part of the improvement policy, you are now ready to plan, carry out (do), and check the results of specific improvements. This three-step process for each improvement is known as the PDC (plan-do-check) cycle. When carrying out this cycle, observe two key points:

1. Make effective and specific improvement plans.
2. Repeat the PDC cycle until you reach the improvement target.

In carrying out improvements, you must be determined to continue until the improvement target is reached. This will be discussed further in Chapter 15.

Make Specific Improvement Plans

To make specific improvement plans that are both economically and technically feasible, you must uncover the *why* and the *how* of the situation. The following guidelines can help in planning effective and specific improvements.

First, if the improvement plan does not make sense or if the improvement effort is plagued with problems, it is usually because the causes have not been clearly understood. Often, improvement plans made without this understanding are themselves difficult to understand.

Second, remember that the causes of minor stoppages are slight defects or combinations of slight defects. It is usually more effective to eliminate these defects by making improvements aimed at increasing precision rather than by remodeling the equipment.

Third, any improvement plan that contradicts scientific theory is doomed to fail. Before taking action, check to make sure your improvement plan makes theoretical sense.

Finally, keep in mind that a large percentage of minor stoppages are caused by a lack of positional accuracy in mechanical devices. Do not rely on visual judgments of precision; instead, use the appropriate gauges to measure and maintain precision.

Examples of Specific Improvement Plans

The following are 30 case studies of specific improvement plans. For the sake of brevity, the results analysis sections have been omitted from these reports. In addition, some of the text has been paraphrased. The intent in including these case studies is not so much to show what kinds of solutions go with what kinds of problems, but rather to illustrate the variety of slight defects that can lead to a single minor stoppage problem. In addition, these case studies illustrate some of the detailed aspects of establishing specific improvement plans.

The reader should recognize that the solutions given here do not apply to all similar problems, nor are they necessarily the best solutions for the problems described. For example, the chamfering of chute connections can be a solution to a problem in one case and a cause of additional problems in another.

Case Study 1. Parts Feeder: Sorting of Incorrectly Oriented Parts

Parts get ejected if they are not correctly oriented when they reach an air jet.

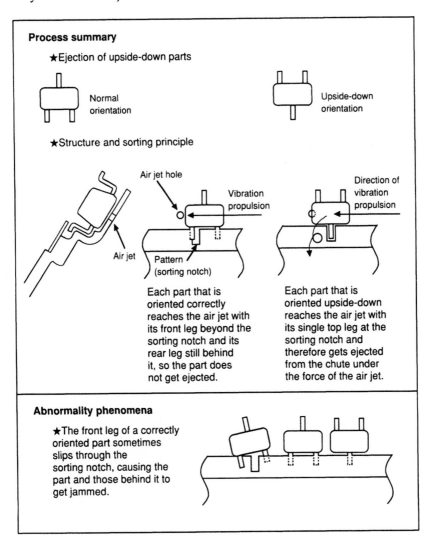

Process summary

★Ejection of upside-down parts

Normal orientation

Upside-down orientation

★Structure and sorting principle

Air jet hole

Vibration propulsion

Direction of vibration propulsion

Air jet

Pattern (sorting notch)

Each part that is oriented correctly reaches the air jet with its front leg beyond the sorting notch and its rear leg still behind it, so the part does not get ejected.

Each part that is oriented upside-down reaches the air jet with its single top leg at the sorting notch and therefore gets ejected from the chute under the force of the air jet.

Abnormality phenomena

★The front leg of a correctly oriented part sometimes slips through the sorting notch, causing the part and those behind it to get jammed.

Main causal mechanism

Dimension X
(the distance between the back edge of the air jet hole and the front edge of the sorting notch) is too small.

The part begins receiving air from the air jet before the front leg has passed the sorting notch.

The front leg gets blown through the sorting notch.

Improvement measure summary

Make sure that dimension X is longer than dimension A.

Make sure that dimension X is not longer than dimension B, since that would prevent upside-down parts from being ejected.

Accordingly, B should be greater than X, which in turn should be greater than A. The optimum value for dimension X based on this theory can be calculated using the following formula.

$$X = 1/2 \, (A + B)$$

After calculating this value for dimension X, locate new sorting notches in the chute according to measurements based on this value.

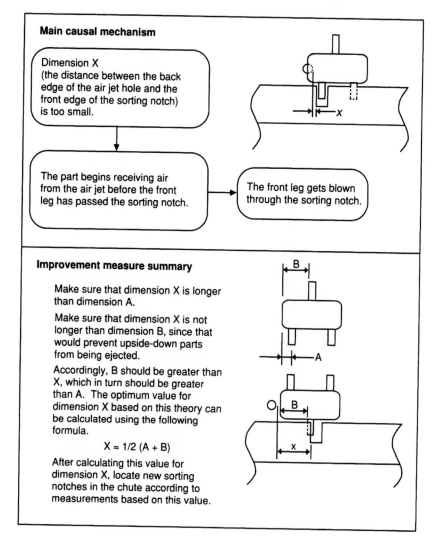

Case Study 2. Parts Feeder: Wiper Angle

Parts get jammed when the wiper angle is too large. If the wiper angle is set according to the theoretical optimum angle of $\tan\theta < 1/\mu$, the parts do not slip smoothly along the wiper edge.

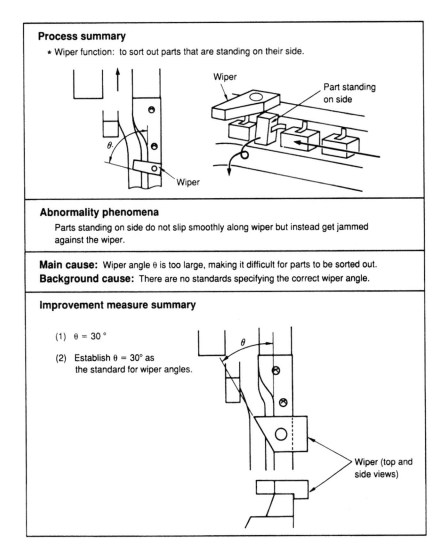

Process summary

* Wiper function: to sort out parts that are standing on their side.

Abnormality phenomena

Parts standing on side do not slip smoothly along wiper but instead get jammed against the wiper.

Main cause: Wiper angle θ is too large, making it difficult for parts to be sorted out.
Background cause: There are no standards specifying the correct wiper angle.

Improvement measure summary

(1) $\theta = 30°$

(2) Establish $\theta = 30°$ as the standard for wiper angles.

Case Study 3. Parts Feeder: Small Parts and Static Electricity

When the parts feeder bowl has been coated, small parts that include plastic materials can accumulate enough static electricity to get stuck in the feeder bowl.

Process summary

Vibrating parts feeder bowl

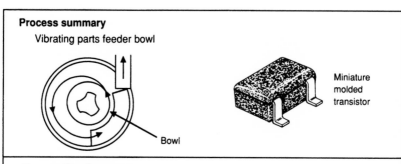

Bowl

Miniature molded transistor

Abnormality phenomena

The transistors stick to the bowl surface and do not get fed to the chute.

Occurrence trends

(1) Tends to occur on days when ambient humidity is less than 40%

(2) Occurs only with transistors made by company M

Main cause: *static electricity.* The parts feeder bowl has an insulating coating to protect the transistors, and this coating contributes to the buildup of static electricity.

Improvement measure summary

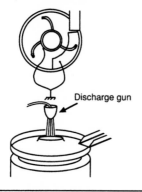

Discharge gun

(1) Grounded aluminum ribbons can be attached to the bowl to disperse static electricity.

(2) To avoid abnormalities caused by ribbon wear, it would be more appropriate for mass-production conditions to use a static discharge gun.

Case Study 4. Parts Feeder: Entanglement of Springs

When springs get entangled in the parts feeder, they continue to move along normally until they reach the exit point, where they get jammed and can cause minor stoppages. The solution was to wind all end coils at least 1.5 times.

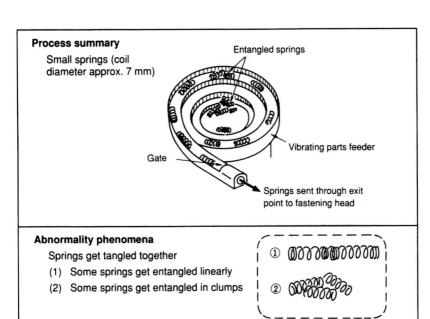

Process summary

Small springs (coil diameter approx. 7 mm)

Entangled springs

Vibrating parts feeder

Gate

Springs sent through exit point to fastening head

Abnormality phenomena

Springs get tangled together

(1) Some springs get entangled linearly

(2) Some springs get entangled in clumps

Springs that are entangled in clumps can be sorted out via a wiper or gate, but those that are entangled linearly pass by wipers and gates and get caught in the shutter at the exit point.

Main cause

Coil ends are wound only 1 time.

Improvement measure summary

Wind coil ends at least 1.7 times to prevent linear entanglement.

Case Study 5. Parts Feeder: Entanglement of Hooked Springs

Hooked springs get entangled linearly, and are therefore able to pass by the gate in the parts feeder, but they get jammed at the exit point, causing minor stoppages.

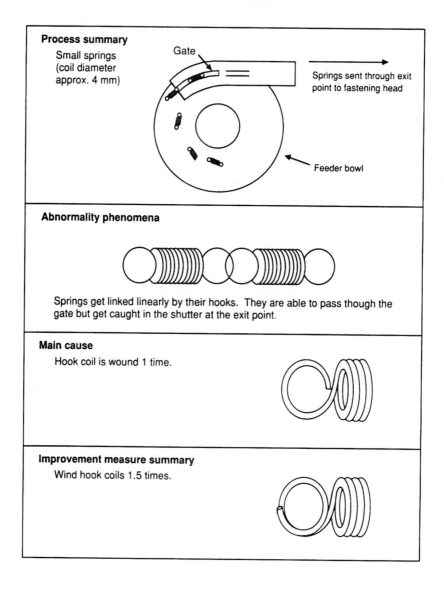

Process summary

Small springs (coil diameter approx. 4 mm)

Gate

Springs sent through exit point to fastening head

Feeder bowl

Abnormality phenomena

Springs get linked linearly by their hooks. They are able to pass though the gate but get caught in the shutter at the exit point.

Main cause

Hook coil is wound 1 time.

Improvement measure summary

Wind hook coils 1.5 times.

Case Study 6. Parts Feeder: Treatment of Entangled Springs

Springs that are bent or entangled sometimes get jammed at the gate. As a solution, the team attached air jets to both sides of the gate to blow away entangled or bent springs.

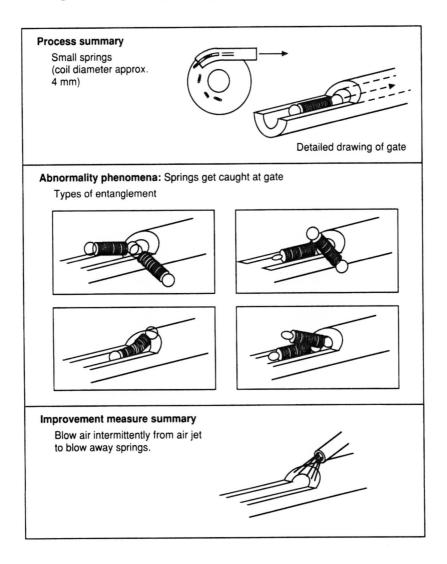

Process summary

Small springs
(coil diameter approx.
4 mm)

Detailed drawing of gate

Abnormality phenomena: Springs get caught at gate

Types of entanglement

Improvement measure summary

Blow air intermittently from air jet
to blow away springs.

Case Study 7. Parts Feeder: Gap Between Feeder Troughs

Small parts sometimes fall into the gap between two segments of the trough and cause minor stoppages. To solve the problem, improvement team members checked the gap between trough segments with gauges.

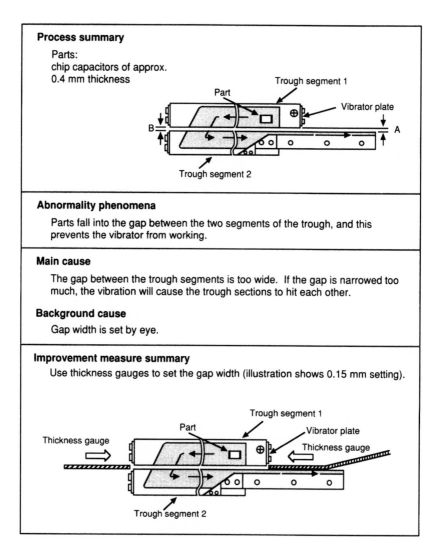

Process summary

Parts:
chip capacitors of approx.
0.4 mm thickness

Abnormality phenomena

Parts fall into the gap between the two segments of the trough, and this prevents the vibrator from working.

Main cause

The gap between the trough segments is too wide. If the gap is narrowed too much, the vibration will cause the trough sections to hit each other.

Background cause

Gap width is set by eye.

Improvement measure summary

Use thickness gauges to set the gap width (illustration shows 0.15 mm setting).

Case Study 8. Chute: Chute Connection Settings

To prevent small parts from getting caught in slight gaps in chute connections, improvement team members used a gauge block to check the connection settings. This eliminated the need to rely on vision and touch for this measurement.

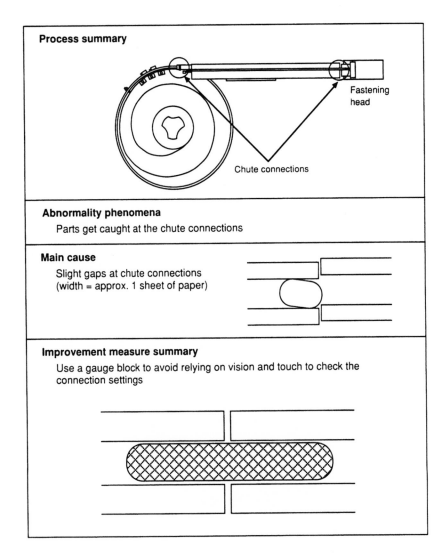

Process summary

Fastening head

Chute connections

Abnormality phenomena

Parts get caught at the chute connections

Main cause

Slight gaps at chute connections
(width = approx. 1 sheet of paper)

Improvement measure summary

Use a gauge block to avoid relying on vision and touch to check the connection settings

Case Study 9. Chute Width and Chamfering of Chute Connections

At chute connection points, the lower chute must be narrower than the upper chute. Even if the widths must be the same, this still requires too much precision in centering the two chute sections.

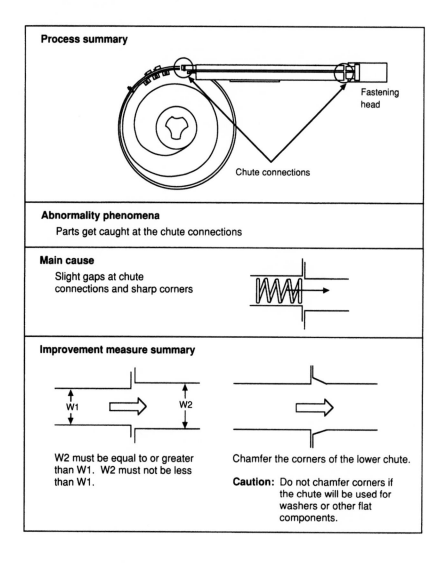

Process summary

Fastening head

Chute connections

Abnormality phenomena

Parts get caught at the chute connections

Main cause

Slight gaps at chute connections and sharp corners

Improvement measure summary

W1   W2

W2 must be equal to or greater than W1. W2 must not be less than W1.

Chamfer the corners of the lower chute.

Caution: Do not chamfer corners if the chute will be used for washers or other flat components.

Case Study 10. Chute: Linearity

Problems often occur when conveyance chutes have curved surfaces or other obstructions to linearity. Straightening these chutes eliminates these problems and makes retooling easier, too.

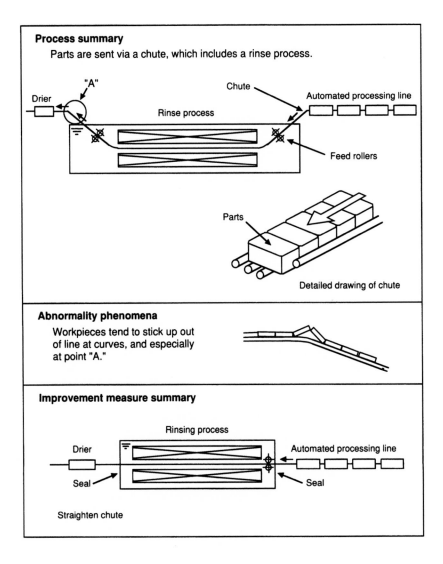

Process summary

Parts are sent via a chute, which includes a rinse process.

"A"

Drier

Chute

Automated processing line

Rinse process

Feed rollers

Parts

Detailed drawing of chute

Abnormality phenomena

Workpieces tend to stick up out of line at curves, and especially at point "A."

Improvement measure summary

Rinsing process

Drier

Automated processing line

Seal

Seal

Straighten chute

Case Study 11. Chute: Parts that Are Too Wide for the Conveyance System

If L is the length of parts in the direction of conveyance, and W is their width in the same direction, there will be a high risk of entangled parts if L/W is less than one.

Process summary

Parts with a width (W) greater than their length (L) in the direction of conveyance can get caught up easily. The following formula was designed to clarify the dynamic conditions required for avoiding such entanglements.

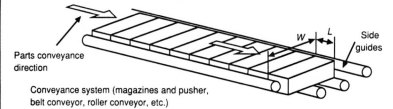

Parts conveyance direction

Conveyance system (magazines and pusher, belt conveyor, roller conveyor, etc.)

Side guides

Dynamic force calculation

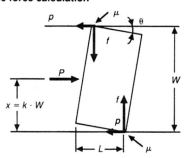

P: Push force against parts
f: Reverse force of entangled parts
μ: Friction coefficient
p: Friction force $= \mu \times f$
θ: Inclination angle (slight gap)
k: Coefficient

| Balance of momentum: | $P \times x = f \times L$ | (1) |
| Push force: | $2 \times p < P$ | (2) |

When $p = \mu \times f$ and $x = k \times W$, according to equations (1) and (2) above.

$$(L/W) > (2k \times \mu) \qquad (3)$$

With ($k = 1$) as the worst possible condition, you arrive at the following conclusion.

Conclusion

The minimum condition (with no safety margin) for preventing entanglement is: $L/W > 2\mu$

Examples: If $\mu = 0.15$, $L/W > 0.3$
If $\mu = 0.25$, $L/W > 0.5$

Case Study 12. Tubular Chute for Feeding Springs

If the inside diameter of the tubular chute is only slightly larger than the outside diameter of the springs, slight unevenness in spring coil winding can result in chute blockage.

Process summary

Compressed springs are fed downward in a line through a tubular chute.

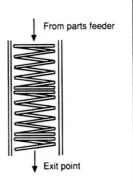

From parts feeder

Exit point

Abnormality phenomena

Springs sometimes get caught in the chute (about 4 springs per 100).

Main cause

Misshapen springs that get caught in the chute are described as having the dimension $(D_0 + d)$. The inside diameter of the chute is D_s and the problem stems from a situation where $D_0 < D_s < (D_0 + d)$.

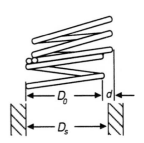

Improvement measure summary

The inside diameter of the chute must be widened by a value of σ, as expressed in the following formula.

$D_s = (D_0 + d) + \sigma$, where σ is about one-half of d.

Case Study 13. Pneumatic Conveyor:
Hose Connection Points for Conveying Small Screws

When hoses are cut by hand, they may not be cut at a clean angle. This leaves burrs on which small screws can get caught at hose connection points.

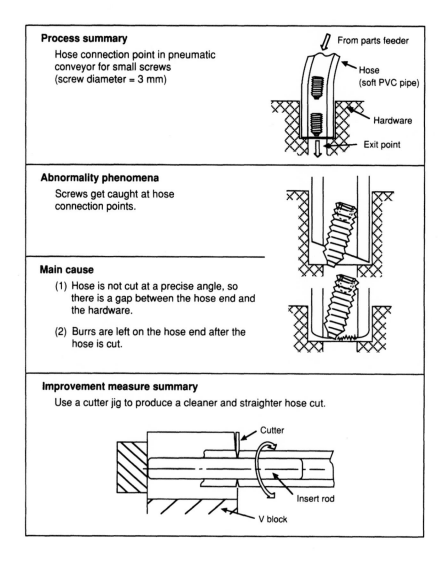

Process summary

Hose connection point in pneumatic conveyor for small screws (screw diameter = 3 mm)

From parts feeder

Hose (soft PVC pipe)

Hardware

Exit point

Abnormality phenomena

Screws get caught at hose connection points.

Main cause

(1) Hose is not cut at a precise angle, so there is a gap between the hose end and the hardware.

(2) Burrs are left on the hose end after the hose is cut.

Improvement measure summary

Use a cutter jig to produce a cleaner and straighter hose cut.

Cutter

Insert rod

V block

Case Study 14. Pneumatic Conveyor:
Width of Hose for Conveying Small Screws

The inside diameter of the hardware inlet must be equal to or greater than the inside diameter of the inlet hose. The inside diameter of the hardware outlet slot must be equal to or less than the inside diameter of the outlet hose.

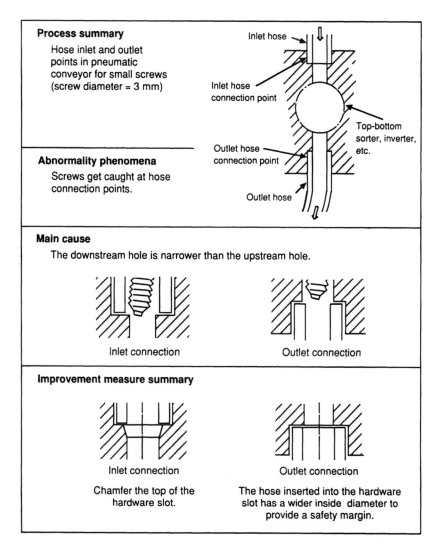

Process summary
Hose inlet and outlet points in pneumatic conveyor for small screws (screw diameter = 3 mm)

Abnormality phenomena
Screws get caught at hose connection points.

Inlet hose

Inlet hose connection point

Top-bottom sorter, inverter, etc.

Outlet hose connection point

Outlet hose

Main cause
The downstream hole is narrower than the upstream hole.

Inlet connection

Outlet connection

Improvement measure summary

Inlet connection

Chamfer the top of the hardware slot.

Outlet connection

The hose inserted into the hardware slot has a wider inside diameter to provide a safety margin.

Case Study 15. Pneumatic Conveyor:
Insertion Mark in Hose for Conveying Small Screws

Screws get caught when the hose is not properly inserted into the hardware slot or when it slips out.

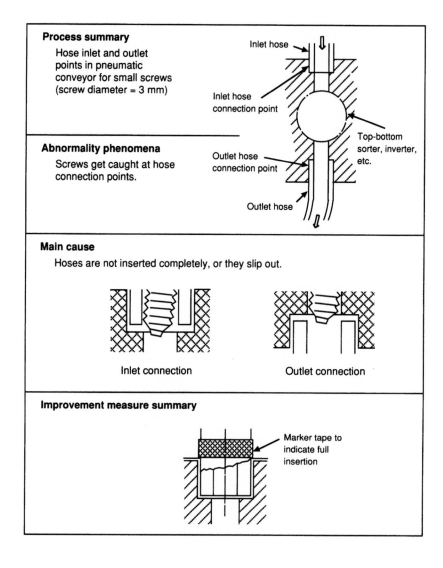

Process summary

Hose inlet and outlet points in pneumatic conveyor for small screws (screw diameter = 3 mm)

Inlet hose

Inlet hose connection point

Top-bottom sorter, inverter, etc.

Abnormality phenomena

Screws get caught at hose connection points.

Outlet hose connection point

Outlet hose

Main cause

Hoses are not inserted completely, or they slip out.

Inlet connection   Outlet connection

Improvement measure summary

Marker tape to indicate full insertion

Case Study 16. Pneumatic Conveyor: Finish Angle at Bottom of Receptacle for Inlet Hose Conveying Small Screws

The incorrect finish angle at the bottom of the inlet hose receptacle produces a gap, and screws can get caught in it. The angle was remachined to a right angle.

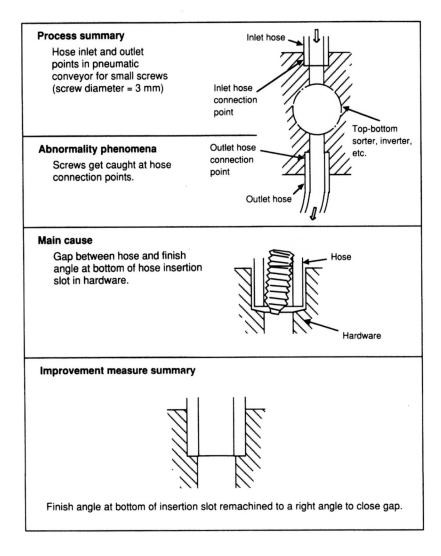

Process summary

Hose inlet and outlet points in pneumatic conveyor for small screws (screw diameter = 3 mm)

Inlet hose

Inlet hose connection point

Top-bottom sorter, inverter, etc.

Abnormality phenomena

Screws get caught at hose connection points.

Outlet hose connection point

Outlet hose

Main cause

Gap between hose and finish angle at bottom of hose insertion slot in hardware.

Hose

Hardware

Improvement measure summary

Finish angle at bottom of insertion slot remachined to a right angle to close gap.

Case Study 17. Pneumatic Conveyor:
Hole Alignment for Conveyor for Small Screws

When the conveyor holes are not aligned precisely, a gap occurs at which screws can get jammed. The problem was solved by setting hole width tolerances and using a gauge bar (an insert gauge) to make and check the hole alignment.

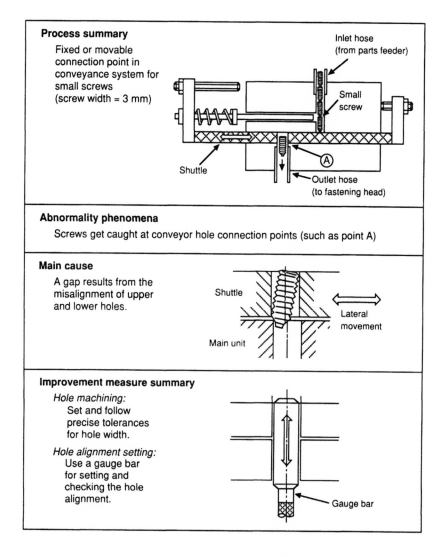

Process summary

Fixed or movable connection point in conveyance system for small screws (screw width = 3 mm)

Inlet hose (from parts feeder)

Small screw

Shuttle

Outlet hose (to fastening head)

Ⓐ

Abnormality phenomena

Screws get caught at conveyor hole connection points (such as point A)

Main cause

A gap results from the misalignment of upper and lower holes.

Shuttle

Lateral movement

Main unit

Improvement measure summary

Hole machining:
Set and follow precise tolerances for hole width.

Hole alignment setting:
Use a gauge bar for setting and checking the hole alignment.

Gauge bar

Case Study 18. Pneumatic Conveyor: Chamfering of Connection Points in Conveyor for Small Screws

The lower part of the conveyor hole connection was chamfered to prevent occurrence of slight gaps between upper and lower pneumatic hose connections. Gaps can be caused by hole diameter errors or errors in the disassembly, assembly, and setup of the conveyance device.

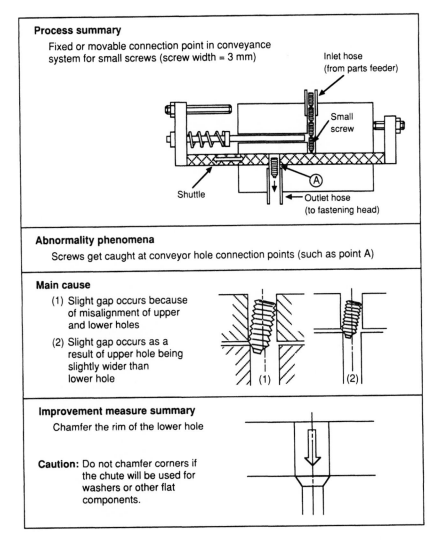

Process summary

Fixed or movable connection point in conveyance system for small screws (screw width = 3 mm)

Inlet hose (from parts feeder)

Small screw

Shuttle

Outlet hose (to fastening head)

Abnormality phenomena

Screws get caught at conveyor hole connection points (such as point A)

Main cause

(1) Slight gap occurs because of misalignment of upper and lower holes

(2) Slight gap occurs as a result of upper hole being slightly wider than lower hole

Improvement measure summary

Chamfer the rim of the lower hole

Caution: Do not chamfer corners if the chute will be used for washers or other flat components.

Case Study 19. Robot: Problems When Many Pick-up Operations Are Performed from the Same Pallet

Sometimes, minor stoppage problems can be the result of positioning errors that occur when the robot picks up many parts from the same pallet.

Process summary

During the automated assembly of cylindrical parts (approx. θ 5 × 12 λ), a robot picks up parts that are supplied on a pallet.

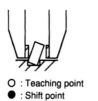

Part
Robot finger
Pallet

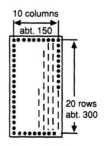

10 columns
abt. 150
20 rows
abt. 300

Abnormality phenomena

An error occurs when the robot finger shifts from the correct position (teaching point) relative to the target part. The amount of position shift is shown by the broken lines in the figure.

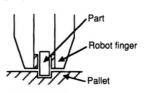

O : Teaching point
● : Shift point

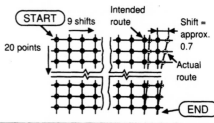

START   9 shifts
20 points
Intended route
Shift = approx. 0.7
Actual route
END

Main cause   The robot arm makes large curving motions near the main unit, which causes the accumulation of small shifts away from the teaching points.

Shift function: This function enables the robot arm to move three-dimensionally in parallel motions using integral multipliers based on the teaching point data.

Improvement measure summary

Change from 9 shifts per teaching point to 4 shifts to reduce shift errors.

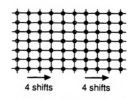

4 shifts   4 shifts

Case Study 20. Magazine: Magazine for Horizontally Conveying Thin Flat Objects

Chamfering the rim of the downstream parts of connections easily leads to jamming when the conveyed parts are thin flat objects that are moved horizontally. For this reason the team decided to install either a high-precision straight connection or one with just a slight tapering of the downstream part of the connection.

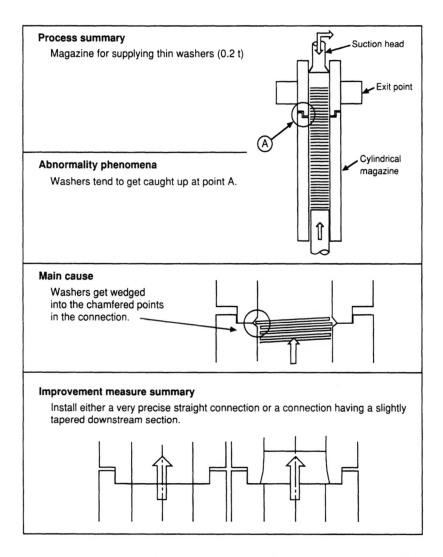

Process summary

Magazine for supplying thin washers (0.2 t)

Suction head

Exit point

Cylindrical magazine

Abnormality phenomena

Washers tend to get caught up at point A.

Main cause

Washers get wedged into the chamfered points in the connection.

Improvement measure summary

Install either a very precise straight connection or a connection having a slightly tapered downstream section.

Case Study 21. Belt Conveyor: Parts Fall from Gate

A mechanism was needed to keep workpieces that are carried on a conveyor belt from falling off when they reach the gate.

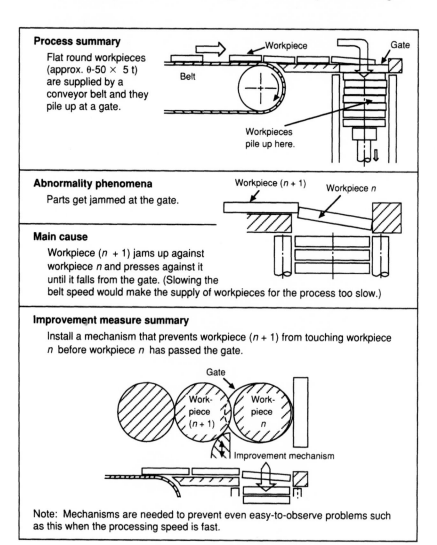

Process summary

Flat round workpieces (approx. θ-50 × 5 t) are supplied by a conveyor belt and they pile up at a gate.

Workpiece

Gate

Belt

Workpieces pile up here.

Abnormality phenomena

Parts get jammed at the gate.

Workpiece (n + 1)

Workpiece n

Main cause

Workpiece (n + 1) jams up against workpiece n and presses against it until it falls from the gate. (Slowing the belt speed would make the supply of workpieces for the process too slow.)

Improvement measure summary

Install a mechanism that prevents workpiece (n + 1) from touching workpiece n before workpiece n has passed the gate.

Gate

Work-piece (n + 1)

Work-piece n

Improvement mechanism

Note: Mechanisms are needed to prevent even easy-to-observe problems such as this when the processing speed is fast.

Case Study 22. Positioning of Workpieces: The Use of Edge Locators

The following examples illustrate various criteria for the use of edge locators.

Summary

Edge locators are used to position parts. They can provide very accurate positioning, but can lead to errors if not used properly. The following are some guidelines to help ensure accurate positioning. These are applicable to cutting and grinding as well as machining and other processes.

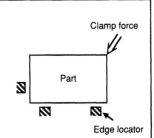

Conditions for stable positioning

(1) Use of three edge locators

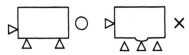

(2) W should be large and H small.

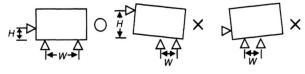

(3) The line of greatest clamping force should intersect points B and C.

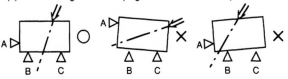

(4) Minimize the area of contact between the edge locators and edges (to minimize the risk of foreign matter entering between them).

(5) If the edge locator covers a corner, ensure that there is a place for burrs or other foreign matter to go.

(6) Make sure the edge locators are strong enough that they do not move under clamping pressure.

Clamping force

Case Study 23. Cutting Debris: Loose Debris from Dry Cutting

When mechanical problems reduce the force of the airflow, cutting debris can settle in corners of the reference surface and remain there.

Process summary

This process uses a rotary index type of automatic machine tool for making bolting holes and countersinks in brass alloy parts. The parts are fed to the process through a magazine and are set onto the reference surface by an auto loader.

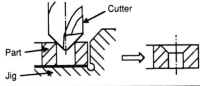

Abnormality phenomena

The sensor that checks the position of the part on the jig detects an error and the machine switches off.

Main cause

Cutting debris remains on the reference surface. Although the combination of an air blower and a suction device are currently used to remove debris from the reference surface, this does not remove cutting debris that occasionally drops from the auto loader arm or other sources.

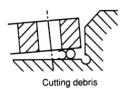

Cutting debris

Improvement measure summary

To completely rid the reference surface of foreign matter, the diameter of the suction port was enlarged.

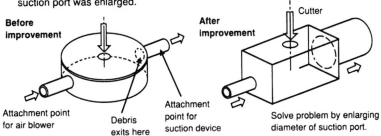

Before improvement

Attachment point for air blower

Debris exits here

Attachment point for suction device

After improvement

Cutter

Solve problem by enlarging diameter of suction port.

Case Study 24. Cutting Debris: Coolant Nozzle Setting

In a process that uses coolant nozzles to remove cutting debris, the team established a standard nozzle layout and accurate measurements for properly repositioning the nozzles each time they are moved.

Process summary

The target equipment is an automated precision cutting machine for small workpieces.

Abnormality phenomena

The accumulation of fine cutting debris causes problems in chucking precision. These problems are automatically detected and the line is then stopped.

Main cause

The positions of the coolant nozzles are changed during retooling and other maintenance operations.

No clear standards have been set for the nozzle locations and direction of spraying.

Improvement measure summary

For each nozzle, establish standard values for location and direction of spray.

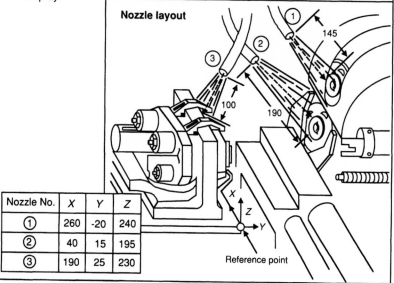

Nozzle No.	X	Y	Z
①	260	-20	240
②	40	15	195
③	190	25	230

Case Study 25. Cutting Debris:
Cutting Debris Gathers on Drill Tips

Coolant sprays do not effectively remove cutting debris from drill tips. The team added a guide bushing as a wiper to aid in the removal of this debris.

Process summary

On an automated machining line that includes precision drilling and tapping processes, an automatic inspection is carried out prior to tapping to make sure that the primary holes were drilled correctly.

Abnormality phenomena

Errors occur because cutting debris accumulates on the inspection pin.

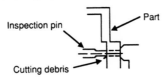

Main cause

At the drilling process, some cutting debris from the drill tip was passed to the inside of the drilled hole, where it remained during the inspection process.

Usually, the spray from the coolant nozzle removes this cutting debris, but occasionally some debris remains and causes problems at the inspection process.

Improvement measure summary

A wiper was added to remove cutting debris as the drill is withdrawn from the workpiece.

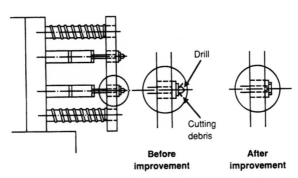

Case Study 26. Packaging: Effectiveness of Suction Pads

To ensure that suction hoses do not kink, the team attached a relay fastener to the operating arm to support the weight of the hoses.

Process summary

This is the first process in an automated packing line for large items (700 mm ×600 mm × 600 mm). The suction pads are used to pick up folded cardboard boxes.

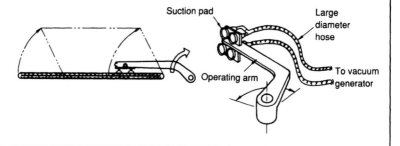

Abnormality phenomena

The sequence is sometimes stopped because of insufficient suction strength.

Main cause

Since the suction hoses are wide and not very flexible, the bends and kinks in them can affect the suction strength so that the pads are unable to pick up the folded boxes.

Improvement measure summary

Attach a relay fastener to the operating arm and use flexible, coiled hoses.

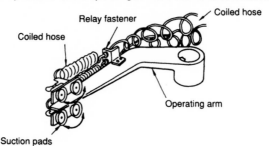

Case Study 27. Packaging: Error Detection Using Photoelectric Sensors

The team improved the stability and sturdiness of the equipment by installing a support to secure the photoelectric sensors and prevent them from vibrating. The sensors are used to check the positions of heavy items (10-20 kilograms) in a high-speed process (cycle time: 20 seconds).

Process summary

The photoelectric sensors detect the position of boxes being raised on the elevator.

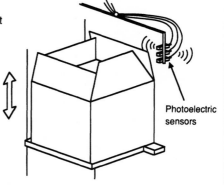

Photoelectric sensors

Abnormality phenomena

Position detection errors occur (resulting in shorter cycle time).

Main causes

(1) The support frame for the photoelectric sensors is not strong enough to prevent them from vibrating and causing detection errors.

(2) The photoelectric sensors first detect the box flaps, so there is some variation in position detection that increases as operating speed increases.

Improvement measure summary

The team installed a stand-alone support channel for the photoelectric sensors to prevent them from vibrating. They also re-positioned the sensors.

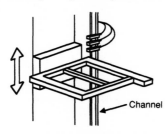

Channel

Case Study 28. Automatic Inspection: Noise

In the automatic inspection of electronic circuit boards, the contact pressure of the power feed rollers must be measured and checked during periodic maintenance.

Process summary

This is an automated memory write and inspection process for printed circuit boards. The boards are conveyed to an inspection stand, where power is supplied through power feed rollers located underneath the stand.

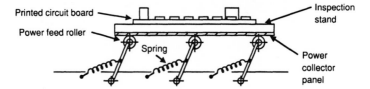

Abnormality phenomena

Electrical noise is produced and occasionally causes the process to stop.

Main cause

Weakness in one or more of the springs attached to the power feed rollers. This causes inadequate roller contact pressure, which causes noise to occur in the power charge.

Supporting cause

Accumulation of dirt on the power feed rollers and power collector panel.

Improvement measure summary

(1) Periodic measurement of spring strength

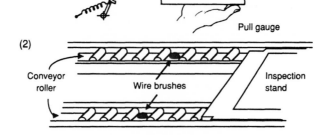

Case Study 29. Motor Timer: Operation Errors

Operation errors occur an average of once every 2,000 operations. The team chose to use an electronic timer instead of a motor-driven timer to ensure the high reliability required for unstaffed nighttime operation.

Process summary

Automatic ejection of large workpieces (e.g., θ -500 × 5,000 λ) after processing.

Workpiece

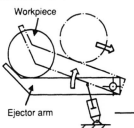

Ejector arm

Abnormality phenomena

The ejector arm fails to operate about once every 2,000 operations. After being restarted, it continues to operate normally. Nothing seems to be wrong with the electrical circuits.

Observation of progressive phenomena

A video camera was mounted to record nighttime operation. An abnormality in the motor-driven timer was discovered during the fifth night of recorded operation.

Main cause

Occasionally, the timer resets itself too quickly.

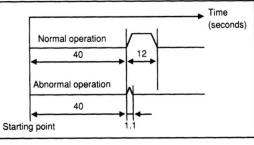

Improvement measure summary

(1) Replace the motor-driven timer with an electronic timer.

(2) To further improve reliability, use a feedback sequence to signal arrival at next process.

Note: This example describes a process in which thorough improvements were needed to completely eliminate quality defects, equipment problems, and handling errors, the goal being to permit unstaffed nighttime operation. The team was able to solve the particular problem described here by observing a type of minor stoppage that is very difficult to reproduce.

Case Study 30. Pneumatic Cylinder: Rod Tip Connection Using Linear Guide

Operations were obstructed very often because the linear guide did not ensure parallelism with the central axis of the cylinder.

Process summary

The linear guide serves to guide the operation block, which is driven by an actuator in a pneumatic or hydraulic cylinder.

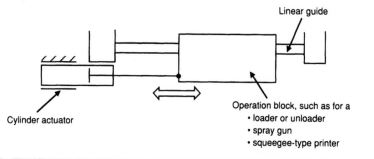

Linear guide

Cylinder actuator

Operation block, such as for a
• loader or unloader
• spray gun
• squeegee-type printer

Abnormality phenomena

The operation stops while in progress, the speed is unstable, and the cylinder undergoes accelerated deterioration (short rod packing life, etc.).

Main cause

Because the cylinder is fixed in place and the cylinder rod is directly attached to the operation block, any lack of parallelism between the linear guide and cylinder prevents smooth operation.

Improvement measure summary

Use a floating link or rotary support where the cylinder rod connects to the operation block.

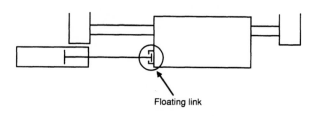

Floating link

14

Step 8:

Do Follow-up Management

This step consists of performing the follow-up measures necessary to maintain those gains that resulted from reaching the target value and completing the improvement theme. For the short term, follow-up management is centered on standardizing the improvements and enforcing those new standards. Over the long term, however, standardization alone may not be enough to prevent backsliding.

STEP 8-1: STANDARDIZE

Strictly speaking, follow-up management begins the moment each improvement goal is reached. Once the effects of an improvement have been confirmed, begin to revise the operating standards to incorporate the improvement. Accordingly, think of standardization not as something to be considered only after reaching the improvement target, but as part of the overall improvement process.

Strength lies in maintaining improvements

Main Target Areas for Standardization

There are three main target areas for standardization:

1. Operation standards for settings
2. Equipment PM operation standards
3. Quality standards

Operation Standards for Settings

The concept of operation standards for settings is not a very familiar one, but having a group of such standards is especially important when implementing minor stoppage improvements. These standards encompass a wide range of equipment settings, such as chute widths, chute positions, stroke positions, limit switch positions, photoelectric switch positions, timers, pneumatic and hydraulic pressures, velocities, and so on.

Regardless of what these operation standards are called, they exist in factories in one form or another. The problems are found in the detailed aspects of those standards. To build a new

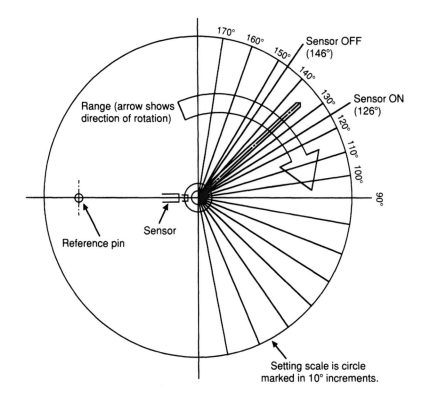

Figure 14-1. Phase Indexing-Sensor Setting Standard

set of standards to maintain improvements, the slight defect phenomena must once again be analyzed. Figure 14-1 shows an example of one such operation standard.

Equipment PM Operation Standards

Since minor stoppages occur most often in automated equipment, maintenance is a key part of follow-up management. In this case, PM refers to *preventive maintenance* (maintenance to prevent breakdowns) and not to *productive maintenance*, which includes post-breakdown maintenance. For equipment that tends to have minor stoppages, the only real kind of maintenance is the preventive kind, because post-breakdown maintenance should be thought of as repair work rather than maintenance work.

Once a successful improvement has been made and the results have been confirmed, determine the maintenance management points for the target equipment. These become the management points for subsequent PM activities. Specific areas of concern for maintenance activities might include hydraulics, lubrication, pneumatics, mechanical precision (static and dynamic), the electrical and control systems, or a thorough cleaning of functional parts of the equipment. Ideally, the maintenance duties should be divided among the operators and the equipment technicians (mechanical, electrical, and electronic).

The maintenance activities should be placed in the proper scheduling category. These categories include routine maintenance, periodic maintenance, maintenance that can be done during equipment operation, and downtime maintenance.

It is important to distinguish between periodic and routine maintenance. For purposes of this book, periodic maintenance activities are defined as those performed at an interval of once each month or less often. The line is drawn at one month because the checklists and PM tables that are tools for PM management often use monthly time divisions.

Figure 14-3 shows an example of a PM management table for keeping records of daily maintenance based on the results entered in the routine maintenance checklist. This table can also be used to record estimated output for each day, which can then be erased and replaced by actual results. Figure 14-2 lists the categories for maintenance periods and job duties using abbreviations.

In principle, use separate PM checklists for each set of job and period categories.

Figure 14-3 shows an example of a routine maintenance checklist, while Figure 14-4 is an example of a periodic maintenance checklist.

The preceding was a description of how periods are established for standardized periodic maintenance. However, establishing such periods is not enough in itself for the management

Person	Period	During Running Time = R	During Stop Time = S
Operator = OP	Shift = S	OPSR	OPSS
	Daily = D	OPDR	OPDS
	Weekly = W	OPWR	OPWS
	Monthly = 1M	OP1MR	OP1MS
Equipment Div., mechanical maintenance = MM	Weekly = W	MMWR	MMWS
	Monthly = 1M	MM1MR	MM1MS
	Every 3 months = 3M	MM3MR	MM3MS
	Every 6 months = 6M	MM6MR	MM6MS
Equipment Div., electrical maintenance = ME	Weekly = W	MEWR	MEWS
	Monthly = 1M	ME1MR	ME1MS
	Every 3 months = 3M	ME3MR	ME3MS
	Every 6 months = 6M	ME6MR	ME6MS

Note: Abbreviations such as OP1MR are used to show the job and maintenance period categories.

Figure 14-2. "Who" and "When" Categories for PM Checks

of continuous periodic maintenance. For example, your table may show that a certain maintenance task is to be done once every three months, but it does not name the actual months. Everything should be as explicit as possible to ensure that everyone can use the table without confusion. A periodic maintenance management table should show the actual months during which long-term (once a year or twice a year) maintenance tasks are to be done. The person responsible can erase the estimated entry and fill in the actual results after completing the maintenance task.

Person	Time	Site No.	Maintenance or Check Item	Minutes	1	2	3	4	5	6	7	8
			Signature									
			Supervisor's signature									

Legend

(1) Person — OP = operator, PM = PM technician, etc.
(2) Time — SRT = starting time, STP = stopping time, WSRT = weekly starting time, MSRT = monthly starting time, etc.
(3) Site No. — Site No. as shown on machine
(4) Minutes — Standard time required (in minutes)

Figure 14-3. Routine Maintenance Checklist

Year		Month				Target equipment					(Machine No.)												
9	10	11	12	13	14	15	16	17	18	19	20	21	22	23	24	25	26	27	28	29	30	31	

(5) Order of entry — Enter person and time data in the checking order.
(6) Weekly and monthly periods — Enter estimated periods as circles.
(7) Check results 4 = OK
         X = NG
         ⊗= OK after adjustment or repair

High Reliability Production Research Center PMCL-4

Division: _____

Note: Use separate pages for different job/period pairings.

No.	Check item	Checking Method	Description	Symbol	Tolerance
	Leaky air hose connection at whetstone head		Brush off the 4 air hose connections and use soap solution to clean out air hose at 6 kg/cm² pressure.	A	Clean until all bubbles are gone.
				B	
				C	
				D	
	Clean lubricant tank		Drain tank completely and rinse out any sediment, air-blow until dry, then fill with new oil.		Use 4 liters of Makoma 33 oil (red label)
	Machine level		Use precise liquid level gauge (1 dev. 0.02 mm/m) to check reference planes (top surface of spindle head).	X	0.02/m
				Z	"
	Check verticality of bed slide surface		Use the tail stock as the origin point, support a test bar from the center, then use a dial gauge placed on the table.	A	0.02 per 800
				(Vertical)	
				B	"
				(Horizontal)	
	Play in operating arm	+1000g / −1000g / This figure shows X axis only	For each of the X, Y, and Z axes, observe dial gauge readings with operating arm in home position and with weight applied in each direction along the axis.	X direction	0.2
				Y direction	0.2
				Z direction	0.2
	Roller rotation resistance		Set the specified amount of weight on the roller and turn the roller to check rotation.	1	W = 5g
				2	"
				3	"
				4	"
				5	"

Figure 14-4. Periodic Maintenance Checklist

Equipment:		Job:			Period:			Page:			
Month/year		Month/year		Month/year		Month/year		Month/year		Month/year	
Treatment		Treatment		Treatment		Treatment		Treatment		Treatment	
Before	After	Before	After	Before	After	Before	After	Before	After	Before	After

Figure 14-5 shows an example of this kind of periodic maintenance management table.

Quality Standards

Sometimes, the causes of minor stoppages include quality problems in procured parts or at upstream processes. If these causes had a direct relation to the improvement results, those improvements should be included as items for standardization, a process that must include revision of the current quality standards and guidelines.

Education and Training in Standard Operations

Factory employees need to receive training in the maintenance of new standards. It is not within the scope of this book to describe such courses of instruction, but their importance is certainly worth noting. It is also worth noting that organizations for education and training have sometimes included quantitative evaluations of worker skills.

STEP 8-2: MANAGE TARGET MAINTENANCE VALUES

In the improvement process, it is important to set clear target values and to achieve those targets by repeating the improvement cycle. But it is also very important to set clear goals for ongoing maintenance management and to monitor its results.

Obstacles and Key to Maintaining Improvement Results

It was previously mentioned that over the long term, standardization alone may not be enough to prevent backsliding. In today's factories, product runs are getting shorter and shorter. Major changes in process conditions are made when changing product models, and these changes pose the biggest obstacles to

Improvement

Steady, ongoing improvement

maintaining improvement results. The records show that maintenance of improvement results has generally been problem-free except in cases where process conditions are changed substantially to accommodate a product model change. When such large changes are made, there has been some backsliding on improvement gains in almost all cases. The main reason is that initial defects are introduced as part of the new process conditions, and as a result, abnormalities occur that make it impossible to maintain the improvement standards. Abnormalities will even occur despite the maintenance of those standards. In such cases, the key is to carry out the improvement once again. By nature, improvement is an ongoing process of steady efforts to make things better.

Key Points for Management of Maintenance Target Values

The following points are useful for maintenance management.

				Year _____					Dept.
No.	Equip-ment	Job/Period Category	Mainten-ance Item	April			May		
				1-10	11-20	21-30	1-10	11-20	21-31
1									
2									
3									
4									
5									
6									
7									
8									
9									
10									
11									
12									
13									
14									
15									
16									
17									
18									
19									
20									
21									
22									

Name of person filling   Person responsible for   Person responsible for
out table   displaying table   updating estimates
_____   _____   _____

Figure 14-5. Periodic Maintenance Management Table

Team _____   Sheet No. _____

	June			July			August		September	
1-10	11-20	21-30	1-10	11-20	21-31	1-10	11-20	21-31	1-10	11-20

1. The production department is responsible for the continuous implementation of this management table.
2. This table is to be used for maintenance tasks having periods of once a month or longer.
3. Enter job and period information in abbreviations, such as MM3MS.
4. Enter the maintenance items using the same units as in the periodic maintenance checklist.
5. Enter estimates as circles.
6. Fill in estimate circles in red ink to indicate completion.
7. Be sure to enter the following information on the management table.
   (1) Name of person filling out table
   (2) Person responsible for displaying table
   (3) Person responsible for updating estimates
   (4) Site where table is to be displayed

Display
site _____

High Reliability Production Research
Center PMCL-3

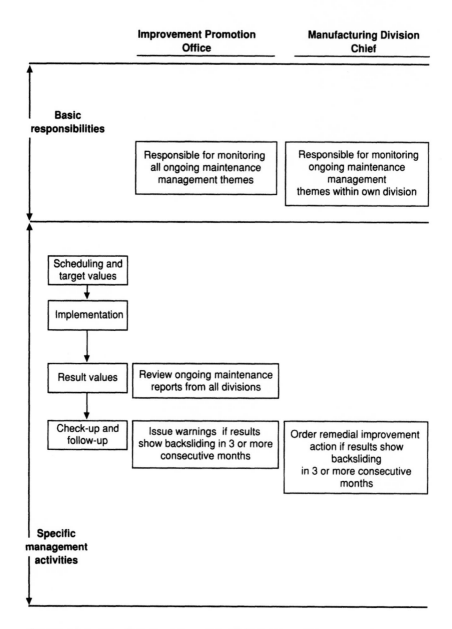

Figure 14-6. Key Points of Ongoing Maintenance Management

Manufacturing Department Chief	Improvement Theme Leader
Responsible for carrying out all ongoing maintenance management themes within own department	
Responsible for carrying out all equipment PM activities within own department	Responsible for carrying out ongoing maintenance management activities concerning own theme
Check ongoing maintenance management target values	Establish ongoing maintenance management target values
	Carry out maintenance activities to reach ongoing maintenance management target values
	Keep result statistics
Action to be taken against backsliding: When substantially different process conditions due to product model changes make it difficult or impossible to perform ongoing maintenance activities, concentrated remedial improvement measures need to be taken, with the support of the company organization.	

Make Clear Assignments of Responsibility

The responsibility for ongoing maintenance management belongs to the department (or production line) related to the target process or equipment. At the factory level, the responsibility for monitoring result statistics belongs to the head of the related improvement promotion office. These are just typical examples of where certain responsibilities lie; other arrangements are possible. The point is that such assignments of responsibility must be made as clearly as possible.

Keep Result Statistics and Confirm Target Values

First, recognize that keeping result statistics should not stop when the improvement is completed, but should continue afterward. These statistics basically concern monthly records of MTBF results. At the very least, they should be checked by the relevant department chief, and it is also a good idea to have them reviewed by the factory improvement promotion office.

Second, it is vital that target values for ongoing maintenance be established and confirmed. The easiest way to do this is to simply establish the improvement target values as the ongoing maintenance values. However, more ambitious people have recognized that setting slightly higher values is a good way to encourage further investigation into slight defects and further improvement. As previously mentioned, improvement is an ongoing process of steady efforts to make things better.

Take Action Against Backsliding

When results indicate that backsliding has occurred on earlier improvements, the first thing to do is to determine whether the new standards have been followed. This job normally belongs to the relevant department chief.

If, for some reason, the standards cannot be maintained, go back to step 5 (*analyze results*) and plan another improvement to correct the situation.

If the relevant section chief is unable to carry out remedial improvement efforts on behalf of the factory improvement promotion office, the matter should be brought before the factory management committee, which can determine how the remedial improvement will be made.

Figure 14-6 summarizes the key points of ongoing maintenance management.

15

Promotion of Improvements

The steps toward reducing the frequency of minor stoppages are based on the results of improvement measures encountered during years of consulting work. Unfortunately, knowing these steps is not all that is necessary to make successful minor stoppage improvements. To reach the kind of substantial improvement goals proposed in this book, improvement teams must also be spurred on with encouragement at every step in the process. Without such encouragement, the chances of success are slim. In this book, *promotion* is the term used to describe this type of encouragement.

The principal role of the improvement team leader (and of the related department manager, too) is to function like the engine that propels the train toward its destination.

Key Points for Promoting Improvement

In today's factories, both the active and supporting members of improvement teams will invariably realize the importance of actually making the improvements. And, naturally,

Promotion

their enthusiasm increases when they have seen good results in the past. Everyone would like to see improvements directed at minor stoppages, since they are the kinds of problems frontline factory operators and technicians must deal with daily. With this in mind, consider the following two points as the keys to promoting improvements.

1. Determination to reach the target values.
   Strong determination is the wellspring of strong leadership. Success depends upon whether the improvement team leader is truly determined (in action, not just in words) to reach the target values of the improvement theme.
2. Steadfast leadership until the goal is reached.

Even when the improvement project runs into tough snags, the leader must provide even-tempered and strong leadership to see the team through to success.

Promotion Methods

The promotion of improvement gets into full swing upon completion of the first two steps in the improvement process (*initial planning* and *measure MTBF*).

Often, members of new improvement teams will be flabbergasted at the goal of reducing minor stoppages to $\frac{1}{20}$ their current levels. They wonder how such an improvement can be made. Sometimes, it helps if the leader explains the need for improvements, how they will be carried out, and the specific role of each team member. Such promotion methods could include the following:

- Explain the difficult conditions imposed by today's business environment and what each team member's department must do to help keep the company on the right track.
- Point out the various problems caused by minor stoppages at the team's process or line, and cite statistics that show just how much actual loss these stoppages are causing.
- Describe the goals of the upcoming improvements and explain why these goals must be achieved.
- Express a personal determination to lead the team all the way to success in reaching the improvement goal.
- Explain to the active group members that they are being asked to make improvements to eliminate current slight defects. They will be sure to set aside enough time to do this.
- Make sure the team understands that they are not being asked to work alone. They will have the support of the improvement promotion office and related technical staff

in solving technical problems as well as process quality or equipment problems that chiefly concern upstream processes.

- Explain to the supporting group members that they must work hard to eliminate the many slight defects that have arisen as a result of imperfections in the work performed by the technical staff. The supporting members are there to help the active members all along the road to success, not just here and there.
- Explain that there is always a way to succeed in making improvements.

Minor stoppages are errors made by automated equipment. Although they may occur frequently, they are not the type of errors that result in a steady stream of defective products. The frequency of their occurrence depends on the operation cycle time and other factors, and once people analyze and understand the detailed circumstances that cause them, they can drastically reduce their frequency.

Ongoing Promotion of Improvement

At step 7, improvement promotion is aimed at applying the PDC cycle in slight defect improvements. No matter how hard it gets, the team must be continually encouraged to achieve their improvement goal. One way to accomplish this is by holding promotion meetings about once each month.

The leader must be a constant participant in this ongoing promotion of improvement. The following text describes what *ongoing promotion* means.

Continuous Series of Promotion Meetings

Some things that seem simple enough to explain and accomplish turn out to be quite difficult. Monthly meetings are easy to schedule, but busy work activities and pressures often make them very hard to enforce. However, success or failure in holding a continuous series of promotion meetings is often a decisive indicator of the team leader's determination.

Figure 15-1. Promotion Meeting

Investigation of Causes

When the investigation of causes is inadequate, there is little chance of success. That is precisely why the investigation of causes using results analysis is such an important part of the process. Whenever an improvement project fails to achieve good results, the first place to look for mistakes or shortcomings is the improvement team's investigation of causes. There are two key points to remember concerning this investigation.

First of all, if the minor stoppage phenomena exist, so do their causes. It only remains for you to identify them. This is the attitude you must adopt. Second, if you cannot find the causes, it is because you have not looked closely enough for them. When fishing for detailed causes, use a fine-mesh net.

Improvement Policy

After the investigation of causes, the next most important part of making minor stoppage improvements is establishing an improvement policy, as described in Chapter 7. Thorough improvement becomes impossible if you allow yourself to fall into either the habit of accepting current conditions or the habit of thinking that adjustments are improvements. Do not be complacent and resign yourself to the current state of affairs. Things do not have to be the way they are. Making adjustments to correct minor stoppages is nothing more than making repairs; it has nothing to do with improvement.

Use a fine-mesh net when fishing for causes

Sources

JIS shinraisei yogo Z8115 (Japanese Industrial Standards glossary of reliability Terms, No. Z8115), Japan Standard Association, 1981.

Nakaigawa, Masakatsu. *Sukiru kanri semina tekisuto* (Transcript of skills management seminar). Japan Management Association, 1971.

Shinraisei kanri benran (Reliability management handbook). Nikkan Kogyo Shimbun-sha, 1964.

Index

CPSIA information can be obtained at www.ICGtesting.com
Printed in the USA
LVOW060725240312

274481LV00004B/53/A